ONE DAY YOU [...]
MORE DISA[...]
BY THE THINGS YOU
DIDN't DO THAN BY
THE THINGS YOU DID
DO.

DON't LET LIFE PASS
YOU BY.

I WILL ALWAYS BE
EXTREMELY PROUD OF
YOU.

LOVE
YOUR DAD

ENDORSEMENTS

I'm honored to tell the story of my dad in the must-read book *That's My Dad!* It's an amazing peek inside the lives of people you may have heard of before, who share in such a personal way details about their dads—the good and the bad. Participating in the book made me realize once again how blessed I've been to have a father who was ever present in my life—a father who always guided me by living the life lessons he preached, with faith and family as his foundation.

GRETCHEN CARLSON
Award-winning journalist and host of Fox News
Channel's *The Real Story with Gretchen Carlson*

In this day and age when one of the world's greatest, most vital institutions—that of fatherhood—is under attack, Joe Pellegrino and Joe Battaglia have done us a huge favor. By capturing such varied accounts of fatherhood experiences, they have touched on the topic in nearly every way imaginable, and in so doing, show us the importance and necessity of dads.

CHRIS BROUSSARD
Internationally known NBA analyst for the ABC and
ESPN television networks as well as an award-winning
journalist for *ESPN The Magazine* and ESPN.com

In *That's My Dad!* authors Joe Battaglia and Joe Pellegrino have shown us that no matter who you are or what you have achieved, one thing is true about everyone: fathers matter deeply in the lives of their children and ultimately in the life of our nation. Our culture often mocks fatherhood in various ways, but there's nothing funny about the number of broken lives left behind by absentee and abusive fathers. Our children deserve better, and this book affirms the necessary role of fathers or a father figure in the life of each child.

RITA COSBY
Emmy-winning TV host and best-selling author

Why read this book if you're like me and you never had a father you could look to as a model of faith and love and blessing? Because, like you, I *want to be* the kind of father this book talks about and models in the life stories described here! Even if you come from a broken family or background like me, you can find *real* examples of godly, imperfect, but totally committed fathers pictured here that you can follow. And one day you'll hear those awesome words, spoken with love from your children, "That's *my* dad!"

JOHN TRENT, PHD
President of StrongFamilies.com and author of
The Blessing and *Life Mapping*

This book is not only entertaining, it is also beautiful, honest, and tremendously important. That's because fatherhood is the most tragically underestimated and misunderstood issue in our culture today. Please be a part of changing that by reading this book and sharing it with your friends.

ERIC METAXAS
New York Times best-selling author of
Seven Men: And the Secret of their Greatness and
host of the nationally syndicated Eric Metaxas Show.

My friends Joe Battaglia and Joe Pellegrino have come up with a truly practical and personal approach to fathering in *That's My Dad!* They have cleverly woven together insights into the lives of interesting individuals with personal stories of their own to highlight the role of fathers (and lack of fathers) in the lives of successful people. As the executive director of the Fatherhood CoMission, I'm always looking for resources that we can recommend. This is a must-read book for anyone who wants to better understand how to honor their father.

MITCH TEMPLE
Executive Director, Fatherhood CoMission
President, Temple Consulting

Our culture today is at a crossroad. There is an epidemic of broken families that have littered our streets with broken children. Absentee and noninvolved fathers who have abdicated their roles as leaders and mentors are taking their toll on the most vulnerable of victims—our children. At All Pro Dad, we know all too well the statistics about children from fatherless homes and seek to reverse that through our work. In *That's My Dad!* Joe Battaglia and Joe Pellegrino clearly speak of how important fathers are in the lives of their children and why fathers matter! Dads should read this book with their kids!

MARK MERRILL

President of Family First and author of
All Pro Dad: Seven Essentials to Be a Hero to Your Kids

There is no clearer view into the heart of a father than through the eyes of his children. *That's My Dad!* gives us an extraordinary gift of heartwarming stories from national world changers about their dads. Serving as a fathering guidebook to those who want practical wisdom about how to turn their heart goals into action, this book is one of the most powerful fathering books I've ever read. It doesn't just tell; it shows how to be an invested parent. If every dad in America took to heart the lessons taught by these mentor dads, it would positively change the landscape of our entire country.

DR. MICHELLE WATSON

Author of *Dad, Here's What I Really Need from You:
A Guide for Connecting with Your Daughter's Heart*

From my early days in professional baseball to working with college kids afterward, one thing was always obvious: the caliber of any individual is shaped tremendously by the presence or absence of a father in that young person's life. In *That's My*

Dad! my friends Joe Pellegrino and Joe Battaglia illustrate how vital that father figures are and how the ultimate Father, God, can help fill a void left by absentee fathers. It's a book well worth reading.

BOBBY RICHARDSON
Former New York Yankees star second baseman

That's My Dad! is an insightful look at the important part fathers play in the lives of their children as told from the perspective of many leading figures from the world of sports, broadcasting, and ministry. It's a book meant to be shared with those important father figures in your life!

DELILAH
National radio host

"Behind every successful child is a good dad" is not only one great quote from this book, but could be a summary truth of *That's My Dad!* You simply have to read this book! You'll love the stories of real fathers who have fathered their children well, launching strong, successful, and values-driven adults into the world, who are making a positive impact in people's lives. Your vision of the importance of great dads will skyrocket as you read this valuable work.

DR. PETE ALWINSON
Executive Director, Forge
Pastor Emeritus, Man in the Mirror

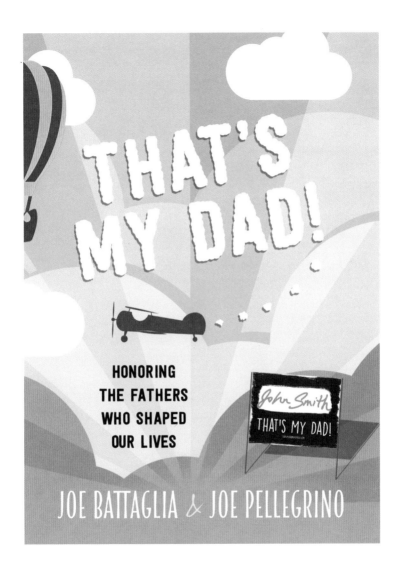

THAT'S MY DAD!

**HONORING
THE FATHERS
WHO SHAPED
OUR LIVES**

John Smith
THAT'S MY DAD!

JOE BATTAGLIA & JOE PELLEGRINO

BroadStreet
PUBLISHING

BroadStreet Publishing Group, LLC
Racine, Wisconsin, USA
BroadStreetPublishing.com

THAT'S MY DAD
HONORING THE FATHERS WHO SHAPED OUR LIVES

ISBN-13: 978-1-4245-5220-7 (hardcover)
ISBN-13: 978-1-4245-5221-4 (e-book)

Cover design by Chris Garborg at garborgdesign.com
Typesetting by Kjell Garborg at garborgdesign.com

Printed in China
16 17 18 19 20 5 4 3 2 1

DEDICATION

JOE PELLEGRINO

To my beautiful wife, Bethanne. Thanks for providing me with three incredible blessings and helping me to be a better dad. To Joey, Jenny, and Jordan. A man could not love and respect his children more than me. And to my Savior and Lord, Jesus Christ, all I can say is THANK YOU!

JOE BATTAGLIA

To my always charming wife, LuAnn, and beautiful daughter, Alanna. I am grateful for a family that has given me much joy and accepts my failures with equal status of my successes. And with whom we walk down the broken road together, committed to each other despite the difficulties.
I am a blessed man!

FROM BOTH OF US

To the memory of our dear friend and mentor David Swanson. David is the reason we know each other today, and we are forever grateful to him for that introduction. And much more.

ACKNOWLEDGMENTS

We would both like to acknowledge the one person who allowed us to even approach this subject and write this book in the first place—that is the greatest role model ever of a father-child relationship: Jesus Christ Himself. As a Son, He gave us a look at God the Father and essentially said, *Here's how this father-child relationship works best.*

CONTENTS

FOREWORD

BY KEVIN MCCULLOUGH

No one should ever be without a dad.

Saying such immediately puts one at odds with the social scientists, new-wave politicians, laboratory academics who want to endlessly speculate, and sadly even in some church circles now.

But it's true.

The effect of a father in a child's life is immeasurable. When put into the context of a loving marriage and a supportive home, the present and attentive father makes the children in that home exponentially less likely to abuse drugs, question their sexuality, commit criminal activity, be in less than stable relationships, drop out of school, and be a part of other undesirable outcomes.

The stories in this book are not just about children with memories of a dad who was present. They are stories of the deep and lasting impact a father's presence made in the formation of his child. This was personally encouraging to me as I hope it will be to you.

Every dad I've had has abandoned the truth he knew and eventually the son that was his. My paternal father abandoned his faith, my mother, and myself when I was eighteen months old. My adoptive and legal father walked away from his faith in my midtwenties. Both came as devastating losses to me, a man who desired to become a father like those in this book—of deep and lasting impact.

Now with three sons (one adopted) and my precious daughter, my desire grows ever deeper. In the pages of this book, perhaps you, like me, will take great heart in the fact that fatherhood is never outgrown.

The opportunity to shape, impact, form, grow, and most importantly, love the child that bears your likeness, name, and legacy never runs out.

In the twinkle of their eyes before they speak, in the enthusiastic discoveries of their early life, in the waves of disappointment from their first exposure to cruelty, in the heartbreak of love gone bad, in their struggle to assert themselves in a life they are attempting to navigate, and in the moments when they admit they needed you all along: your importance never ends.

None of us who've had a child that we held as a baby will ever tire of walking into a room, the family kitchen, a little league sports games, graduation ceremony, the wedding reception, or any number of other occasions and hearing, "That's *my* dad!"

That moment of a child's pride ... it makes everything worth it!

Kevin McCullough is the nationally syndicated host of "The Kevin McCullough Show" and "*LIVE*" Saturdays (9–11 p.m. EST), ranked as eleventh most listened to talk host in America by *TALKERS* magazine. Kevin is also a weekly commentator to *America's Newsroom* on the Fox News Channel.

INTRODUCTION
DADS MATTER!

You've probably heard the old adage, "Nothing breeds success like success." We often chuckle at this, but the truth of the statement is obvious. Success is not often achieved alone. Successful people only achieve success because someone else is usually there cheering them on, whispering in their ear that they can do it, and loving them through the difficult times that are necessary to shape the skills of each successful person.

The reality is that we often achieve success not for the sake of success itself, but for the sake of the one who inspired us, believed in us, and loved us enough to care and invest in our lives. To be truly valued, success must be shared. So let's create another adage to the above statement: "Behind every successful child is a good dad."

What fathers say will often determine their child's way. The one common denominator of many of society's ills—pornography, human trafficking, abortion, rape, murder, alcoholism, teen suicide, and incarceration—can be traced to absentee fathers. The US Department of Health indicates that 63 percent of youth suicides are from fatherless homes, and that 90 percent of all homeless and runaway children are from fatherless homes too. Not only that, but the Center for Disease Control suggests that 85 percent of all children who show behavior disorders come from fatherless homes, and *Justice and Behavior* states that 80 percent of rapists with anger problems come from homes where a father is absent.[1] Fatherless homes contribute to the national dropout rate among high school students too, revealing that 71 percent of all high school dropouts come from homes where a father is absent.[2] From these statistics, it is easy to see that men who have abdicated their roles as fathers is the single greatest problem in society today.

In this book we will look at the impact of fathers in the lives of highly successful individuals. To compete at the professional level of any field of endeavor requires not just skill but the confidence to stand the stress, and the mental toughness required to be successful. Many men and women have natural skills, but many of the people written about and quoted in this book would be the first to say that without the affirming love and support from their fathers, or from some father figure in their lives, they would not have achieved the level of success that they enjoy today.

We have interviewed many great athletes, celebrities, and business leaders to get their insights on what their dads did to guide them to be the people they have become today, and we have tried to encapsulate their stories in a way that shows the importance of fathers to their success as individuals and how they contribute to society.

At times, though, a loving, involved father is not present in the home, even for many successful people. We interviewed two individuals who either had no father or had an abusive father. And yet, they still had someone in their life that replaced their

1 Raymond A. Knight and Robert A. Prentky, "The Developmental Antecedents and Adult Adaptations of Rapist Subtypes," *Criminal Justice and Behavior* 14 (Dec. 1987): 403–426.
2 National Principals Association Report on the State of High Schools, accessed Jan. 28, 2016, www.fathersrightsdallas.com/tag/national-principals-association-report-on-the-state-of-high-schools/.

nonexistent father with someone to encourage them, believe in them, and be the father in their lives.

And for those who had no fathers in their lives, this is a book about forgiveness. We can still follow the biblical admonition of honoring our fathers by forgiving them, and releasing ourselves from the chains of bitterness, anger, and resentment that do more to hold us down than lift us out of our pasts to secure our futures.

In each chapter that follows, it is our intention to identify the power of true fatherhood and the difference it makes in the lives of children. Each chapter will focus on a central theme embodied by the type of father described, and then enlarge on that theme to illustrate important life lessons, which will be depicted through a mix of exclusive interviews, questions, personal stories, and life principles.

All of us want to, or at least yearn to, stand up and shout, "That's my dad!" Join us to see how we can become the dads our children need and will want to honor.

Joe Battaglia & Joe Pellegrino

My daughter, Alanna, and me,
Joe Battaglia.

Celebrating our 27th wedding anniversary at Yankee Stadium!
Pictured from left to right, Jordan and Joey (sons), Jenny
(daughter), Bethanne (my wife), and me, Joe Pelligrino.

Jerry Girardi

THAT'S MY DAD!

THATSMYDADMOVEMENT.COM

1

JOE GIRARDI

THE FATHER AS MAJOR LEAGUE TEACHER

BACK STORY

Joe Girardi has been the manager of the New York Yankees since 2008, guiding the Yankees to their twenty-seventh World Championship in 2009. He has grown from a little-known journeyman catcher to one of baseball's premier managers, being universally liked and respected for his well-spoken and intelligent demeanor.

Joe was an all-state baseball player in high school in his hometown of Peoria, Illinois, and attended Northwestern University where he earned a bachelor's degree in industrial engineering. After having been named as a three-time All

American and two-time Big Ten selection for his athletic abilities, he broke into the Major Leagues in 1989 and played fifteen seasons with the Cubs, Rockies, Cardinals, and Yankees. He was a three-time World Champion player with the Yankees in 1996, 1998, and 1999.

After retiring from baseball in 2004, he became a commentator for the YES Network. Then, in 2005, Girardi left the broadcast booth to get back in the game as the manager of the Florida Marlins and guided the team to the wild card spot that year. His work with the Marlins earned him the National League Manger of the Year Award in 2006. He then returned to the YES Network in 2007 for one year before accepting his current position as manager of the New York Yankees.

THE INTERVIEW

New York Yankees manager Joe Girardi has been to the World Series as a player with the Yankees in 1996, and then he led the Yankees to the World Championship in 2009 as their manager. But if you ask him, the real champion in his life was his father, who instilled in him the habits and traits that led to his success as both a player and a manager.

Joe's childhood was similar to other working class families in Peoria, Illinois. He was the fourth of five children, with a sister who was right in the middle of four boys. He says, "We were very close as a family. My parents worked hard, but I never felt like they didn't have time for us."

Joe uses one word to describe his father—hardworking. "My father worked three jobs to support us. He was a salesman during the week, and then a bricklayer on the weekend. He would take me with him to the job and I'd mix the mortar, carry the bricks, etc. And he would bartend some nights too. But he also had time to coach our basketball teams, and be there for us.

"Like when I went to Northwestern University. The fall semester would start at the end of September, so a lot of my friends would already be in school. I'd still have a month or so before I would leave, so my dad would feed the pitching machine and I would hit. You know, every day for an hour or so."

Joe described his relationship with his dad as being close. That closeness would help him relate to his ballplayers later on in the big leagues. "I followed my dad around everywhere he went. As I said, I worked with him on the weekends. He was always there for us. He showed us how important it was to make time for us. So I made sure that I was there for my teammates. Relationships are important."

He also credits his dad with teaching him something that was vital to his career as a major league ballplayer—mental toughness. "He demanded a lot from us," Joe recalled. "He taught us toughness. When I'd play my father in basketball, he would box me out—he wanted me to fight back. He wanted to instill in us a toughness to never give up and to find a way to beat him. He was not a dad who was just going to let you win. He was going to make you work, and he was going to rough you up and make you, in a sense, fight back. And I think that's a valuable lesson."

The old adage of learning being caught, not taught, seems to apply to how life lessons were learned in the Girardi household. Joe's dad taught more by example than anything else. "When I think about my father, there are so many values that he taught me," Joe stated. "He taught me the value of a dollar. He gave me my first one-hundred-dollar bill. I worked two days, really hard for eight hours or ten hours a day. I'd come home filthy, but he paid me. He said, 'This is the value of a dollar.' He taught me the value of hard work, of perseverance, the value of fighting back, and the value of the way you're supposed to take care of a family and be there for them."

Being there for the family was especially important to Joe's dad who exemplified how Joe should treat his own wife. Joe's dad was a servant and took care of Joe's mom, especially after she was diagnosed with cancer when Joe was only thirteen years old. Joe said, "She was given three months to live and she lived six more years. My father was a servant. Even though we didn't have a lot of money, he always wanted the best for my mom, for her to feel like she was a princess. He would never let her do any physical work—he would take care of everything around the house and anything that required heavy lifting. He was always there for her, to open the doors, make sure there was gas in the cars—that sort of thing. He was a great example."

Life in the Girardi family was not all work though. There were also a lot of fun memories too, like wrestling and fishing. Joe said, "My dad would wrestle my brother and me at the same time. And all the basketball, football, and baseball we played in the backyard—I'll never forget that. And fishing was always a blast."

One fishing story in particular stands out in Joe's mind. "During Lent, my father would always go fishing, and we'd have fried catfish on Fridays. One time, he went fishing with a friend at four in the morning and they were home by eight o'clock because he had to go to work. My buddy Ricky, who lived down the street, and I decided that we would try to help my dad clean the fish. We were like seven and eight years old at the time. We found every cleaning detergent in the house and poured it in the bucket to clean the fish. We really thought we were helping my father out. We're lucky we didn't blow up the house."

Like most dads who take pride in their kids when they do well, Joe's dad was no different. "My father was very proud of his kids, and was not afraid to boast about it. We used to tell him, 'Dad, Dad, be quiet, be quiet.' He was not a real vocal guy. You know, he would say, 'Come on, Joey.' But he was not the kind of father who would try to tell us how to do a lot of things. He was just there to support us."

Joe stated that his dad's legacy "was the success of his kids. My two oldest brothers are doctors. My sister is a math professor in South Carolina, and my younger brother is a CPA. When I think about my father, he did a great job on the values he instilled in us. He would make us get up on the weekends and clean the restaurant at six o'clock in the morning. Those were good lessons and I'm forever grateful because there's no way I would ever be here if not for my father." Joe then went on to say, "My dad taught me so many lessons by just being himself, and not necessarily by trying to teach me lessons. I'm trying to pass that along to my kids."

Joe's experience with his dad helps him relate to many of the young players he deals with now as a manager; young men who did not have a father's influence like Joe. "I think about all the wonderful times I had with my father and everything he taught me," he said. "It has to be difficult when you don't have a father around. The thing that you hope and pray for is that these young men have good men around them who can teach them the things that a father would teach. I do the same thing for my kids when I'm gone during the course of the season. I try to put good men around my children, people who have values and who will demand a lot from them and expect a lot from them. And I look for that in my kids' coaches too—that they have the same type of people like my father was."

Joe's favorite verse is James 1:2–4, where James writes about the joy of facing trials and how the testing of faith develops perseverance. Verse 4 in particular says, "Perseverance must finish its work so that you may be mature and complete, not lacking anything." "That's all life is, really," Joe stated. "People often think life is supposed to be easy. It's not. It's a grind. It's hard. But you have to be joyful in those situations and remember how good we really have it."

Joe Girardi clearly understood that his father exerted an influence in his life that was worth emulating.

THE STORY: THE MALL TRIP (BY JOE BATTAGLIA)

In this generation, fathers are needed more than ever before to offset the onslaught of influences that would negatively impact our children. These influences are so subtle, so cloaked in popular causes, that we've failed to recognize them for what they truly are. The mantra of an amoral society is that there is no more right or wrong in setting standards of morality, because there is no one truth.

I became acutely aware of this scenario in a rather strange way—by shopping with my daughter about ten years ago. At first this sounds rather innocent, but a closer look revealed something more insidious.

While we were at the mall, my daughter asked to go into a hip, fashionable store for teens to buy a shirt. It must have been more than twenty years since I'd set foot in that store. As I entered, I stopped dead in my tracks. I thought I was in the wrong store—that I'd accidentally walked into an X-rated video establishment. Pictures of half-naked young women (probably not much older than my daughter) lying on top of equally undressed young men adorned the walls.

After spending my life in marketing and communication, there was no mistaking what those images and messages were meant to communicate to all who came through the doors. The message was clear—our culture has sacrificed the innocence of our youth on the altar of sexual glorification. It's no longer about selling clothes; rather, it's more about selling our souls. We decry the way our wives and daughters are disparaged over their body images and seen as sexual objects, yet we promulgate the lifestyles and clothing lines that lead to the very thing we denounce. We have become a schizophrenic society.

But wait, the story did not end there.

My daughter knew me all too well. She knew I'd likely say something and not merely slip away into the night, momentarily decrying the decadence of the situation and then doing nothing. As I stood in the line waiting to pay for the shirt, I grew more mad by the minute. Let's just call it righteous indignation.

As I approached the counter to pay, I observed the young man and young woman who were standing there to service us. They were probably around nineteen or twenty years old. I placed the shirt on the counter, and then informed the young man that I was really offended by the display on the walls. "Please pass my comments on to the manager," I insisted.

Of course, I didn't stop there either, even though my daughter, who was embarrassed by my approach, was turning quite red. So I asked the young man, "How do you feel about working in this environment, particularly working alongside a young lady?" Then I asked the young lady, "How do you feel about all of this? Are you offended, even a little bit? Does this promote the wholesome way in which you'd like to be perceived by the young man working alongside you?"

I guess it was the journalist in me that needed to ask the obvious questions, at least as I saw them.

As my daughter muttered under her breath, "Dad, they don't care," the young man eyed me and said, "I wish my father cared as much." That was his exact quote, which I'll never forget. "I wish my father cared as much," he said.

As we left the store, my daughter sighed. "You know he had to say that," she insisted.

"No," I replied, "he could have said any number of things, like, 'I'll tell my manager.'"

To this day I'm convinced he said what he said because it was on his heart to say it. I suspect that, in this young man's heart, rarely did he see evidence of a man standing up for what he believed in to protect his child from the increasing moral ambivalence that is suffocating our youth with sexual indulgence beyond their ability to handle or even understand it.

In that clothing store, maybe the message was about sexual revolution or that young people have a prevailing mind-set of openness toward sex. Who knows? All I do know is that messages are intentional, and a father can alter the destiny of his children by challenging the prevailing mind-sets of the day to teach them by example and by his words. Joe Girardi is proof of that.

THINK ABOUT THIS

In Deuteronomy 11:18–19, Moses says this to fathers, whom he addresses as the teachers of their households: "Fix these words of mine in your hearts and minds; tie them as symbols on your hands and bind them on your foreheads. Teach them to your children, talking about them when you sit at home and when you walk along the road, when you lie down and when you get up."

God gives men the responsibility to father their children. It's not enough to bring children into the world and only care for their physical and emotional needs. There is a spiritual need that all children have that must be addressed, and God asks us as fathers to meet that need. By nature, all fathers are teachers. Some are absent and some are reluctant, but children will learn *something* from us, even if it's nothing at all. The question is, what do we want them to learn, and from whom do we want them to learn it?

As Joe Girardi stated, and as my (Joe Battaglia) daughter experienced that day at the mall, a father will be the teacher by his actions, his love, and his verbal opportunities to communicate character and truth in everyday experiences—when we sit at home, when we walk along the road, when we shop at a mall, or when we do manual labor. Every experience is an opportunity to teach our children.

THE QUESTION

Who was your favorite teacher and why did you feel so strongly about him or her?

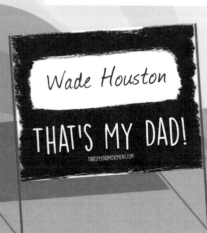

Wade Houston

THAT'S MY DAD!

THATSMYDADMOVEMENT.COM

2

ALLAN HOUSTON

THE AUTHENTIC FATHER

BACK STORY

As a man of faith and strong family values, Allan Houston lives his life with a determination to utilize his success as a professional athlete to help others, while also continuing to grow a variety of entrepreneurial interests. Allan is the assistant general manager of the New York Knicks, and he has also served as an international ambassador for the NBA, a spokesperson for the National Fatherhood Initiative, and an ESPN analyst.

Before his retirement in the fall of 2005, the two-time NBA All-Star was touted as one of the "purest shooters" in the NBA, finishing his career as one of the NBA's all-time greatest long-range shooters, and one of the all-time leading scorers in Knicks history. But for all of his accomplishments, he is especially proud of being named one of The Sporting News' Good Guys in Sports (four times), and helping Team USA bring home the gold medal in the 2000 Summer Olympics games in Sydney, Australia.

Through the success of his philanthropy, Allan was named Father of the Year by the National Fatherhood Initiative in 2007, Social Entrepreneur of the Year by Tulane University in 2008, and he has received the President's Council on Service and Civic Engagement Award from the Obama Administration in 2011.

THE INTERVIEW

Allan Houston is the assistant general manager of the New York Knicks, assuming that role after many years as a standout NBA All-Star with the Detroit Pistons and the New York Knicks. Yet if you were to ask him his pick as the All-Star in his life, he readily points to his father, whom he sums up in two words— love and integrity. "I think these words best describe my father," he said. "My dad was a totally selfless type of person who was just always thinking about others. I think the word that bridges those together would be authentic."

There was nothing fake about his dad at all, stated Houston. "I mean just totally an authentic, transparent, loving man. I mean, he'd give you his last sip of water. Everything about him was about love. He modeled it. He modeled everything he said."

Houston grew up in Louisville, Kentucky, in a sports family. His dad was a high school basketball coach, so basketball and the life of a coach and sports was all they knew while growing up. His mother worked in the financial aid department at the University of Louisville. "She's a very bright woman," Allan proudly stated. "She's a very loving person, the type that when you meet her you feel like you've met your second mom."

The Houston family lived in a lower-middle-class part of Louisville in Allan's earlier years, moving to a different part of town when his father accepted an assistant coaching job at the University of Louisville when Allan was just seven years old. "The school and the area was much different, and we were probably one of three or four black families in the neighborhood once we moved to that part of the city. So there was me, plus my two younger sisters."

Houston remembers that his dad treated all the kids the same, although Allan smiles when he claims that his younger sisters were the apples of his eye. "We had a traditional family environment, with a very sporadic schedule because my father traveled a lot. So, many of our activities were based around his schedule, from games to practices to tournaments. We basically built our lives around those activities. We would take family trips when families could travel with his team." And with both his parents involved in higher education, there was always a strong emphasis and priority on education. "They set a high bar, a high standard," Allan recalled.

"Another thing about my parents," he said, "was that I never remember seeing them or hearing them raise their voice at each other. After being married nineteen years myself, it makes me even more impressed because you know that conflict is part of the equation. They were consistent in their MO that they we're not going to take out anything in front of the children.

"I saw my dad really love and respect my sisters and my mom," Allan said. "I never remember him raising his voice a lot. I mean, he was stern and he had a way that garnered respect from everyone. Everyone knew he wasn't the type who was high-strung and anxious. He has a calm and calculated demeanor, but he also has a very good sense of humor. If you don't know him, you would not know how funny he is. Everyone just loves him."

His father's influence in Allan's life is obvious in what Houston now does with his foundation to give back to the community. "One thing I learned from him is what you give out is what you get back," Allan stated. "If you give off love and respect, then that's what you're going to get back. Even though some people might rub you the wrong way, just roll with it, because at the end of the day the energy you give off, of love and respect and humility, is going to come back to you."

That love and family atmosphere in the Houston home was welcoming, and his parents made everybody who came into the house feel like family. "Whenever I go home to this day, there's no way the house is going to be just my immediate family," Allan emphasized. "There's going to be someone who played for my father, or a friend they've made along the way. It's just kind of amazing to see the people they have made part of their network.

"Another thing they did when I graduated was to start a trust fund for a logistics and transportation company, which was one of the largest minority-owned truck and logistics companies in the nation for a few years. They've employed a lot of people in the community that way. It's just amazing to see the like-minded hearts of a man and woman come together in this way. This is what we saw growing up."

With all the activity around the Houston household, Allan remembers what he enjoyed most with his dad was simply being with him. "I don't remember one activity in particular. Even just sitting and watching TV with him, just little things that connected us, and that's what I remember most. One time I remember putting a lot of time and energy in putting up a basketball pole with my dad and then just playing against each other. Just being around him in any way, shape, or form, you know, it was just fun."

Since education was so important to his father, Allan remembers some great advice from his dad. "He was mindful of the image and impact we all have, so he'd remind us that what you say, do, and how you present yourself leaves a great impact on others. He really emphasized that and that's what I go by." He went on to say, "*Legacy* is a strong word for us because the phrase he'd left and that he was saying when I got older— he was always saying this to his teams and I always remember, 'You'll never get a second chance to leave a first impression.' He reminded us that we always have an opportunity to impact someone, so we were to be mindful of that and take advantage of it."

Obviously, Allan Houston was greatly influenced by the impact his father had on other people, which he describes as unconditional love. "He modeled God's type of love," Allan stated. "Anybody who needed anything, it was almost impossible for him to say no. He was always extending a hand to someone. I could sum up his life by saying that he was born to help other people. He was born to teach, born to give. It was his heart, it was his calling, it was his spirit."

THE STORY: THE BIKE (BY JOE PELLEGRINO, JR)

There is something special about getting your first real bike. My oldest son experienced that back when he was around six years old. It was Christmastime, and my wife and I decided to buy him a bike. She went to Toys "R" Us to select the right bike for Joey. First she looked at a bike called the Tiger Shark. As I recall, it was a hot-looking metallic blue three-speed ride. The problem was that at $150, it was double what we wanted to pay. She wisely decided to get the bike that was in our budget, and once she purchased it she asked the girl at the register to have bike assembled as well (I suppose this was a response to my assembling skills).

A few days later my wife asked me to pick up the now-assembled bike. I picked it up and brought it home. When my wife saw it, however, she said that it wasn't the bike she bought. Instead, it was the bike she originally looked at, the one that was double our budget. Now what? What should we do? It was a few days before Christmas when I brought the bike home, so we decided to give him the bike and if he really liked it we would find a way to pay the difference.

Needless to say, he loved the bike so I knew what I had to do. My son and I got in the car and drove to Toys "R" Us, and went to the customer service desk. I explained to the girl at the desk what had happened. I told her that we had purchased one bike but when we picked it up they gave us another, better bike. She asked me what I wanted her to do, and so I told her I wanted to pay the difference, which apparently was funny because she started to laugh. She then excused herself to speak to her manager who was about a hundred feet away.

Then, like a scene out of *Seinfeld*, we saw them pointing, talking, and laughing, which I am sure was at our expense. The girl was laughing the whole walk back to where we were. She then said, "Look, we can't believe you came back, but since it was our mistake, keep the bike."

As Joey and I walked away, I told him, "See how God blesses us when we do the right thing." Now the truth is that while God always blesses us for what He asks us to do, it doesn't always end like this story. But can we put a price on integrity? Sadly, I have in the past and it has come back to haunt me. Remember that it's never wrong to do the right thing.

THINK ABOUT THIS

Think about integrity for a moment. Allan Houston paid his dad the highest compliment by ascribing that character trait to him, and Joey saw that modeled firsthand by his father's actions—one-time decisions that make a lifelong impact. And it all starts by listening to God.

I wonder what Isaac was thinking when he went with his father Abraham to the mountain and discovered the sacrificial lamb was about to be him. Do you think that integrity had something to do with him complying with his father's wishes to the point where he allowed himself to be tied to an altar as the sacrifice? At what point in that story do you think Isaac put two and two together? Abraham must have exhibited such integrity *before* that incident. Two things had to happen: the first is that Isaac would go with his father to the mountain, completely trusting him, and the second is that God would test him like that in the first place.

If Abraham had not proven himself trustworthy and completely devoted and dependent on God, then God would not have put him in that position. We often hear people preach on that passage and the focus always seems to be on Abraham's trust in God. I really believe it's the other way around; that story shows God's trust in Abraham more than Abraham's trust in God.

Integrity has a way of being tested to actually give it meaning. It's one of those definitions that requires an accompanying action in order for it to be clearly understood. It's a lot like love. Love is not love if it is self-contained; it has to be expressed to have definition and power. And the same is true for integrity—if not acted upon, then it's only a noble intention.

Allan Houston's and my dad clearly exhibited the definition of integrity. In a world that seemingly rewards those who strive for self-aggrandizement and moral compromise above selfless service and moral backbone, integrity will stand out like a sore thumb. When we take a stand for doing the right thing, it will, as Scripture says in Psalm 37:6, make our righteousness "shine like the dawn." Let our integrity go before us, and then God will use us because He can trust us as He did with Abraham.

THE QUESTION

Compromise and integrity cannot exist in a structural sense; just ask any structural engineer and he or she will be able to confirm this. Can God trust you with His calling on your life so you will not come apart under stress? What are you facing today that you need to trust God with for the right outcome?

Father's Day is one of those holidays that touches my heart, just because he's not around anymore, and I think about him. The whole family thinks about him. I think the city of Chicago thinks about him, because he was like a father figure to a lot of people around the city...and a lot of people looked up to him.[3]

Jarrett Payton on his dad, Chicago Bears Hall of Famer, Walter Payton

3 "Jarrett Payton on his dad, Bears Hall of Famer Walter," *Chicago Tribune,* accessed Jan. 28, 2016, http://www.chicagotribune.com/sports/chi-jarrettfathers20110617175124-photo.html.

Lee Carlson

THAT'S MY DAD!

THATSMYDADMOVEMENT.COM

3

GRETCHEN CARLSON

THE FATHER OF INTEGRITY

Gretchen Carlson is an award-winning journalist and host of Fox News Channel's *The Real Story with Gretchen Carlson*. She previously cohosted *Fox & Friends* for eight years and served as a CBS News correspondent and cohost of the CBS *Saturday Early Show*. Although Carlson has interviewed the top newsmakers of the day, her favorite interviews focus on the "real" people who make up the fabric of our country.

Gretchen grew up in Anoka, Minnesota, as a violin prodigy, graduated valedictorian of her high school class, and earned her college degree from Stanford University while also studying at Oxford University in England. She became the first classical violinist to win the Miss America title in 1989.

Carlson has received the prestigious American Women in Radio and Television Best Series Award for her thirty-part series on domestic violence, and two National Emmy Awards for her work at CBS News. She serves on the board of the Miss America Organization, and she is a national trustee for the March of Dimes. She's married to sports agent Casey Close, has two children, and currently resides in Connecticut.

THE INTERVIEW

Fox News personality Gretchen Carlson hosts her own daily show, *The Real Story with Gretchen Carlson* from 2:00–3:00 p.m. Monday through Friday. With a career in television news to go along with her Miss America title in 1989, as well as her musical prowess as a violinist, she has distinguished herself in many ways.

The confidence to engage successfully in all these areas goes back to a secure and loving family in her home state of Minnesota. Her father was a major factor in that equation. "My best description for my father would be a man of integrity," she stated. "I don't really know a person who doesn't like my dad. He was an amazing role model for me."

Gretchen's father was actively involved in their hometown of Anoka, Minnesota (which is about fourteen miles north of Minneapolis), better known as the Halloween capital of the world. He carried on the family car dealership business that his father and his father's uncle started in 1919. Gretchen recalls that they started the dealership after another failed business attempt in the potato starch business, which went bankrupt. "Everyone thought they were crazy to start a car dealership. But it succeeded, and it's been in the family that long. My dad took it over after my grandfather died. And ironically, now, my mom is actually running it."

It was her father's handling of running a business and still being committed to his family that impacted young Gretchen greatly. "He was always trying to negotiate that work-family balance. He'd come home for dinner every single night, so we would always have dinner together as a family, which was so wonderful. And then he'd go back to work afterward and get home at nine thirty or ten o'clock, and go upstairs into his bedroom and sit by the TV and have ice cream and chocolate sauce."

Gretchen also lets us know that her father had an amazing sense of humor, along with being incredibly sentimental and emotional. "My dad and I cry at TV commercials together. So that's where I get my emotional side to my personality."

She remembers that her dad was actively involved in their Lutheran church where her mom's dad was the minister. He'd sing in the choir, serve on the church board, and financially help the church. He served in the Kiwanis Club, and he was on the board of the local hospital. "My family was a huge believer in volunteer service, so I learned that from my parents as well. And so I just knew my dad to be somebody who was incredibly involved in the community.

"I certainly had an amazing man of integrity from that point of view in seeing my dad so involved in everything that really shaped my life. I also learned amazing perseverance from him, because during the seventies, when the oil embargo was going on, selling cars was not a great profession to be in. My dad never let on to how tense those moments actually were and probably how close he was to losing the business.

"Eight years ago, when the presidential administration actually took away the car dealerships of some General Motors owners, my parents lost their business in the last round of cuts, which was a horrible time in our lives. My mom and dad fought back and got their business back. And now my mom runs the business. So that's kind of an overview of my dad."

Gretchen went on to say, "I remember watching him when I used to work at the dealership, which is called Main Motor Sales. A disgruntled customer would come in and my dad would handle that person so graciously, and by the time they left they were smiling and shaking his hand. My dad has an amazing knack with people. He has a way of being an amazing conversationalist with people he's never met before."

Gretchen has many childhood memories she holds dear, especially the times that were instrumental in teaching the Carlson kids how to be grateful for what they had. "We took many family trips. We went to Israel through the church three or four times as kids, and learned cultural differences. Whenever we went overseas, we learned how lucky we were to be Americans.

"We also learned humility from my father. He was the most humble man I've ever met, and he taught us to be humble. Once, when I was maybe six or seven years old, we went to a resort with our entire neighborhood. It was so much fun and I won the whole Bingo pot one night, maybe a hundred bucks, which was a lot back then, especially for a young kid. And I remember my dad saying to me, 'Gretchen, the responsible thing to do would be for you to buy ice cream for everyone.' I'll never forget that he made me do that; it was not something I loved at the time but it was a great life lesson later on."

Her dad also had a special connection with Gretchen's music. Her mom was the driving force in her life, but her dad was the one who really understood her music. Before her many competitions, Gretchen would always play for her dad in their living room before she was ready to go. "My dad would nod that I was ready to go," Gretchen fondly remembers. "He would sit there and close his eyes and listen to me and get very emotional. We had an amazing bond with each other. So I didn't learn necessarily my drive and competitive spirit from my dad, but I learned every other aspect in my life that hopefully has made me a whole person."

This bond he had with Gretchen was also illustrated when her mom would ground her for some reason. "Whenever my mom would ground me or be hard on me when I was growing up," she said, "I'd always call my dad at work and say, 'Dad, you know, sometimes she's too strict—you know how I feel.' And he always made me feel like he was listening to me and that he understood me. He would say, 'I know, but we just have to go along with the punishment.' And I'd say, 'But Dad...' and he'd say, 'Well, just this one night you're grounded.' So he always made me feel like he was still strict but that he understood where I was coming from and that meant a lot to me."

Gretchen has a deep regard for marriage, as she's witnessed how her father has treated her mom with utmost respect throughout their fifty-five years of marriage. "My parents are still in love after fifty-five years of marriage. I remember my mom saying to me recently that she loves my dad more every year, and I can see why. My dad, he cleans up the kitchen after every meal. He cleans the house. Now that my mom is the CEO of the business, my dad goes to the grocery store and he does the cooking, actually. He does all the ironing and all the laundry. And he's an amazing gardener. To this day, it's one of the ways in which he relieves stress, and we always had beautiful gardens at our home in Minnesota. My dad is an amazing golfer. He won the national championship for small colleges in his junior and senior years of college, and he still plays. I think that's what keeps him so young at eighty-two years old. My dad is a fast walker, even when we go to Disney World with our kids."

She continued, "I learned so much about marriage from watching my parents. They've been wonderful role models for me. Especially watching a dad who was so involved even before it was customary for dads to be so involved in the raising of the kids."

Gretchen has also needed her father's advice on a number of things, and he's always been there for her. "I remember after I won Miss America," Gretchen recalled. "I was just shocked at how people didn't like me just because, and that was really, really hard to take. When you grow up in Minnesota, there's something called Minnesota Nice, which is just so true. Everyone is so nice to everyone else. We don't even honk horns.

"I remember saying to my dad, 'Dad, I'm so crushed that people automatically don't like me. I don't know what am I going to do about it.' And he said to me, 'You know what, Gretchen? No matter how hard you try, you're never going to get everyone to like you. And so you have to work on those things you think you can change and disregard those you can't.' (This coming from a guy everyone liked, and that's why it was so important for me to hear it from him.)

"It sounds simplistic, but I have to tell you that I think

about that every single day of my life, even today. Being a former Miss America, having blonde hair and working at Fox News, and because I speak openly about my faith, I have a lot of detractors. And so I think about that advice from my dad almost every single day, and it's really gotten me through a lot of tough days. It has allowed me to not waste time on people whom I'm never going to change their minds, and, trust me, there are a lot of those people out there," she explained.

What Gretchen learned about family from her parents has served her well now that she has her own family. "The last chapter in my book is, 'To Whom Much Is Given.' We believe in the Carlson dictum, which is to give back and teach our children. I believe it's the second most important lesson you can give to your children. The first being something else I learned from my parents, which is giving your children a religious foundation. From there, I can go down the line making sure that we have an appreciation of finances and to have what we have. Add to that showing our children cultural differences and going to church and being involved in the community. And all of those lessons I was so fortunate to have had in my life growing up."

THE STORY: THERE'S ONLY ONE WAY
(BY JOE BATTAGLIA)

I had a rather idyllic childhood. Almost Mayberryish. My family had a large piece of land in our little town, maybe eighteen miles from the Lincoln Tunnel and New York City. We had a nuclear Italian family, as my paternal grandparents lived with us. We also had a large garden, almost a minifarm, because my family simply copied what they had in Italy in my hometown of Totowa Boro, New Jersey.

My grandfather would prepare this almost 10,000-square-foot "garden on steroids" with a pitchfork every spring. No mechanical anything for him. No car. No power mower to cut the grass. Just like it was in his little terraced town in southern Italy. It seems that everyone who came from that part of Italy could build anything or fix anything, whether it was with wood, bricks—you name it. I think it was in the DNA; though I'm not sure what happened to my DNA, because I don't have that inherent gifting.

My grandfather built the chicken coup (yes, we had fresh eggs every morning before we could spell cholesterol), the wine cellar, the front and back porches, the retaining walls along the garden, and most of the inside of our home, which was a three-story dwelling like in the old country. And we grew everything imaginable in that rather large garden, spending all spring and summer preparing the soil, planting, and picking. We grew so many tomatoes that we would jar our own sauce, which was an arduous process that took place each August in the basement kitchen. But it paid big flavorful dividends throughout the year when my mom would make such great sauce dishes with our pasta, sausage, meatballs, eggplant parm, chicken parm, and you name it. We ate like kings.

When it was time to pave the large driveway leading to the detached three-car garage, my grandfather was in charge of that too. I was a young boy then, maybe just five or six years old. So when the truck came with the gravel as the foundation for the paving, I was sitting on the back porch watching all this as my grandfather keenly eyed their every move. One thing about my grandfather was that he looked like a Marine drill instructor, with a face that seemed to be hewn from rock and strength like Superman. You would not want to mess with him. He served in the Italian army during World War I in the artillery. Several years ago I was going through some drawers in my parents' home and found medals he had been given because of his action during that war, along with a commendation letter signed by Mussolini himself, prior to Il Duce's ascension to dictator (that document and those medals are now framed and hang in my living room). My grandfather seemed gruff, but he had a soft heart too, which was not too noticeable, if you know what I mean.

As I was watching the laborers dump the gravel for the foundation, the foreman signaled that enough gravel had been dumped. With that my grandfather brought out a ruler to measure the depth of the gravel, with the foreman looking on studiously. My grandfather straightened up and looked the foreman in the eye and said, in Italian of course, that there was not enough gravel. It was short by an inch or two, I forget which. And that started World War III.

My grandfather and the foreman (who was also Italian) began a typical Italian discussion that regular people call an argument. I sat there bemused, having seen a number of these encounters by now in my early age. And then I heard my grandfather say something that I have never forgotten. As the foreman tried to convince my grandfather that this amount of gravel would be sufficient, my grandfather rebuffed him with this comment: "There's only way to do the right thing." Needless to say, more gravel was then laid that met my grandfather's expectations.

I have heard that phrase resonate in my head many times over the years. I hear it when I'm tired and want to take the easy way, and when it would be easier to settle for less than the best in my work, my relationships, and in my service to God: "There's only one way to do the right thing."

I know what Gretchen Carlson means when she would hear her grandfather and father tell her to be her best, and encourage her as she struggled to practice her violin lessons. There was only way to do it right, and that one way is never easy. But it does pay off. You become a virtuoso and you become Miss America—and a successful broadcast journalist, despite all the naysayers who maybe never had fathers and grandfathers like ours. Or, like me, you become a journalist and a broadcaster, and work with those whose messages and projects you are privileged to provide a platform to change people's lives. And you both help to change the world.

THINK ABOUT THIS

Integrity did not seem to help Joseph very much as he languished in an Egyptian prison. Simply, it was his integrity that put him there. He would not compromise his master's trust by giving into Potiphar's wife, who wanted to seduce him. Just think how much easier it would have been to give in and enjoy pleasure rather than run and land in prison, facing possible death.

Lack of integrity often seems to be pleasurable, and a much easier path to take. But it will catch up to you down the road, and usually the consequences are far worse and longer lasting. Joseph found this to be true. While in prison, he correctly interpreted the dream of his fellow prisoner, the cupbearer of the king, who was released soon thereafter. Two years later, that same cupbearer remembered Joseph's gift of interpreting dreams, and told the king about him, which lead to Joseph's release and eventually being in charge of governing Egypt.

One significant thing about integrity is that someone is always watching—like a young girl who would become Miss America, or a young boy who would one day run his own broadcast company and author a book, or a cupbearer in a prison. When you walk with integrity, you never know how your actions will impact your future, mostly when you least expect it.

THE QUESTION

As a dad, understand that integrity will be a wise man's companion through life. And remember that there's only way to do the right thing. What is something that you can make right today? In what areas do you need to do the right thing?

Jack Kemp

THAT'S MY DAD!

THATSMYDADMOVEMENT.COM

4

JEFF KEMP

THE FATHER AS ENCOURAGER

BACK STORY

Jeff Kemp is an Ivy League graduate who played eleven seasons as a quarterback in the National Football League with the St. Louis Rams, San Francisco Forty-Niners, Seattle Seahawks, and the Philadelphia Eagles. He and his father, Jack Kemp (former vice presidential candidate and secretary of Housing and Urban Development), were one of only six sets of father-son NFL quarterbacks.

In 2012 Jeff joined FamilyLife, which is based in Little Rock, Arkansas, as a vice president and catalyst for helping strengthen families. FamilyLife is a national leader in offering resources to build and enrich marriages and families, providing radio outreach and marriage conferences. Prior to joining FamilyLife, Jeff founded and led Stronger Families in the Pacific Northwest from 1993–2010.

Persevering through the highs and lows of the NFL has given Jeff valuable insights on servant leadership, committed teamwork, and overcoming adversity. Today, he passes on those lessons as he illuminates God's blueprints for manhood, marriage, and family. Jeff and his wife, Stacy, have been married for over thirty years and have four sons and two daughters-in-law. He is an avid mountain biker and snow skier.

THE INTERVIEW

Former NFL Seattle Seahawks and St. Louis Rams quarterback Jeff Kemp followed in his father's footsteps. His father, Jack Kemp, was himself a successful quarterback with the Buffalo Bills. After his playing days with the Bills, Jack Kemp entered the world of politics, becoming a congressman from New York and eventually named as the vice presidential candidate alongside Bob Dole and his bid for the presidency in 2000.

Jeff Kemp had much to say about his famous father's role in his life. He uses one word to describe it: lift. "If you think of what wind does on the wings of an airplane or what hot air does on a balloon or what velocity does to throwing a football, it creates lift," Kemp explained. "If you want to use a simpler word, he was an encourager."

Jeff credits national talk show host Bill Bennett as the one who coined the word *lift* to describe his dad at the elder Kemp's memorial service. "He and his wife came out to our house," stated Jeff. "My uncles, aunts, siblings, and mom we're all telling stories about Dad. Bill Bennett was actually telling funny stories to make us laugh. He summed up Dad's life, saying that Jack Kemp was a 'lift.' Wherever he went, whatever the issue, he brought lift. That's what he was in my life—the ultimate encourager."

Kemp fondly remembers how, from the time he was a child, his father would celebrate everything young Jeff would do. "Even if I was a third-string quarterback, and wasn't playing, Dad was still saying that he was proud of me. He'd tell me my day was going to come, to keep working hard, and to keep thinking like a starter. 'You're going to be a starter. I'm proud of you,' he would say."

Jeff remembers his dad calling him after a game one time, "'Hey, I saw you today. You look great.' I said, 'Dad, I didn't get in the game.' And he said, 'I know, I know...I saw you warming up. You're throwing the ball great. You really stand well.' That's an encourager. He would look for the glimmer of light, for the positive, and focus on that. And if there wasn't a positive, he would create a positive because he'd say that this is just the present, and that in the future you're going to be such and such."

One of the things young Jeff would always hear from his father was to remind him that he's a champ and a leader. "Every one of my siblings heard that," he stated. "I heard that hundreds of times. 'You're a champ. Be a leader.' I call them Gideon words because, in the Bible, when Gideon was still afraid, young, and not yet a courageous leader, the angel of God came to him and said, 'Oh Gideon, you are a great and valiant warrior.'

"So the idea is that the angel of God spoke into Gideon the character that he was to become before he actually became it. That was the nature of my dad. He'd keep saying, 'Hey, your day is going to come. I believe in you. You're in the right plan. God has a plan. You're going to be a starter. Think like a starter. I can't wait to see you play.'"

The one downside of all the encouragement Jeff received was that it could become too performance driven. Jeff recalls that "I ended up performing and I ended up achieving. But I was only a starter in the NFL for two and a half years. I never won a championship like him; I didn't run for congress at age thirty-four like him; I wasn't running for president when I was fifty like him. My dad made identity to be more about what God made me to be or do. So I've learned my identity is in Christ and I've had some readjustment, humbling, and clarifying again that my identity is with God just as I am. But it's awesome to have a dad who encourages you."

Jeff acknowledges that although his father was always encouraging him toward excellence, his father loved him whether he was first string or third string, made the team or didn't make the team. Jack Kemp, the politician, was all about having a vision for one's life, a vision for a country, a vision for the poor, a vision for the underdog. "Dad was always uplifting and casting vision. He was a visionary. So the words I'd use to describe him were visionary, encourager, lifter."

Another aspect of how his dad taught his kids was being around the dinner table almost every night. "He would often get home late for dinner, but he'd make sure to be home for dinner," Jeff said. "He'd have my mom keep us up because he wanted to have conversations at the dinner table with congressmen or senators or economists or athletes or whomever he would bring to dinner. He wanted us to hear their ideas. He included us in the adult world of conversation. In a way, he was preparing us to be leaders, to be influencers."

Jeff fondly remembers a particular habit that his father had with little notes. "His initials were JFK, and he'd take little embossed heavy stock cards with the symbol of the United States on it and write notes to us, saying, 'Hey, Jeff, I'm so proud of you. Hang in there. Your day is going to come.' Or he'd quote a Bible verse like, 'Trust in the Lord with all your heart and understanding. In all your ways acknowledge him.' Or some other Proverb or Psalm. That was his way of saying that God is sovereign. Trust Him. He's got a plan. You don't need to panic. Everything's going to work out. So that was my dad's style. He would write those notes and mail them to me when I was in college, or he would put them at our spot at the table. "

While Jeff's dad was truly encouraging to his children and working to save the world, he credits his mom with making the home environment possible for his dad to be as involved as he was in the world of politics. "She made it easy for him to be a good dad by taking care of everything around the house. She was like the shock absorber who took care of whatever was going on with us in our home, work, and school. Dad was mainly the encourager, but didn't roll up his sleeves as much as she did."

Jeff went on to say as he reflected on his father's influence: "I'm only now learning how I need to break free of some of the patterns that I learned from my dad. My mom actually exhibited more sacrificial love than my dad, who exhibited more sentimental love. What I mean by that is although he loved my mom and my family, he loved the feeling and experience of family more than he practiced the verb itself. Love is seeking to invest yourself in another and sacrifice yourself to bring out the best in them, according to their personality and their desires. That's the definition of love."

Jeff definitely knows what his father's legacy is—his family. "On his deathbed," Jeff reminisced, "he flatly stated that he did not want his legacy to be politics or football. He didn't want it to be how well he did in business. He wanted his legacy to be our family and how much God loved us. He believed in the American idea, and the ideals of this nation and the experiment it represented. America could create greatness because it recognized that God gave us our rights and there is great talent in human beings if you unleash it."

THE STORY: WHAT'S ONE MORE?
(BY JOE BATTAGLIA)

As a kid, I would often accompany my father during the summer to his shoe repair shop in East Orange, New Jersey. It was a long day for a boy who would have preferred to be playing baseball with his buddies, but it was also fun to just be with my dad on these occasions.

My father never pushed us to follow in his footsteps as a shoemaker. He always wanted my brother and me to have a college education and have more than what he had, although that little trade put two of us through college and we never lacked for anything that was worth anything. His sole focus was his family and providing for them, and ensuring that my brother and I would have the opportunity to do more with our lives.

After I graduated with my journalism degree from Boston University, I returned home and, through a series of providential events, had the opportunity to launch my own publication. It was a magazine that focused on tying together the body of Christ in the New York metropolitan area, and defeating the mind-set of what I called "the Elijah Syndrome"—Christians bemoaning the thought that they were the lone believer in the New York area, similar to the prophet Elijah sitting under the juniper tree complaining to God, "I, even I only, am left."

Well, this was quite an undertaking for someone with no capital and no distribution platform, armed only with a vision that God had given to me. At that point, I partnered with someone who would become one of the greatest mentors in my life and used his nonprofit organization under which to publish the magazine. That was helpful. The only caveat was that he could not afford to pay me, which could obviously be an issue.

So with a vision in hand, and not much else, I approached my father and explained what I felt I was called to do—except that I would not get paid. I had been working since I was sixteen, and even worked all four years through college so I could help support myself because my father was paying for my college tuition. I thought that following this dream of starting the magazine might not be so well received because of the financial issue.

After explaining to my father the situation, he did not even skip a beat in his response, which is one I will never forget. He simply said in his broken English, "Hey, I took care of you for twenty-two years. What's one more?" That response was his way of really saying to me, "Son, I believe in you and I want you to follow your dream. Caring for you is my calling. My legacy will be carried on through you."

I launched that magazine and, because of it, the following

year I did a story about a radio station in Jersey switching formats to carry Christian teaching programs and a new type of music that would eventually be called contemporary Christian. I was offered a job at that station as a result of that story, which led to everything I have today and all the wonderful things I have been privileged to do and people I have met. This is one immigrant father who selflessly said to his son, "What's one more year?" and helped launch him on a marvelous journey to what he's become today, which included the writing of this book.

THINK ABOUT THIS

Like Jeff Kemp's dad, David had lots of influence, was a leader of his nation, and exposed his son to the most well-known people and influencers of his day. Scripture does not say this, but it might very well be that the home environment of David and all the people Solomon was exposed to early in his life contributed to his legendary wisdom.

Both men made some mistakes; neither of them was perfect. But that did not prevent God from saying that David was a "man after His own heart," and that Solomon was the wisest man who ever lived. David left Solomon a legacy—he left the whole world a legacy. In fact, from David's lineage would come the Messiah. Now that's some legacy.

Jeff Kemp's famous dad had his great platform, entertained the greatest leaders in the world, exposing his son to all of that, much like David. And at the end of his life he could say that his family was more important to him than all of it—or even *any* of it. At the end of his life, Solomon could look at everything that the world had to offer and called it vanity.

Whether it's Solomon's dad, Jeff Kemp's dad, or my (Joe Battaglia) dad, it all comes down to the type of legacy a father wants to leave behind. You could be a king, a congressman, or a shoemaker—it matters little in the economy of the kingdom of God. What matters most is leaving a legacy for your progeny. I think that even Solomon may have proudly pointed to David at some point and said to all of Israel, "That's my dad!"

THE QUESTION

How are you going to "lift" someone's spirit today, especially someone in your family? We all need an encourager in our lives. Will you be that man?

Cecil Rouson

THAT'S MY DAD!

THATSMYDADMOVEMENT.COM

5

LEE ROUSON

THE FATHER AS LEADER

BACK STORY

Lee Rouson is from Greensboro, North Carolina. There he attended Page Senior High School, where he varsity lettered in several sports and was an integral part of the Page Pirate community. He went on to receive a full scholarship to the University of Colorado, where he played football for Coach Bill McCartney. While at Colorado, he became the fourth all-time leading rusher from 1980–84. Everyone agrees that he was key factor in turning the Colorado football program around to become national champions.

Drafted by the New York Giants and playing under Bill Parcells for six years, Lee won two Super Bowl rings while there.

His final year in the NFL was as a starting fullback and tight end with the Cleveland Browns, under the leadership of Coach Bill Belichick, where his career was brought to an unexpected end as a result of ankle injury.

Lee now serves as a director for the mentoring and leadership program at the Mount Olive Board of Education. He is also a board member for Legacy Minded Men. Working tirelessly throughout the community, Lee encourages everyone from the youth to the elderly with the message of hope. He and and his wife, Lisa, have four children.

THE INTERVIEW

Lee Rouson has two Super Bowl rings as a former NFL running back with the New York Giants. He was born in Greensboro, North Carolina, and moved to New Jersey when he was just a child. While in New Jersey, his father met Malcolm X and became one of his bodyguards.

According to Rouson, "Malcolm X pretty much was kicked out of the nation of Islam, so he started an organization called the Afro-American Unity Organization. My father became one of his bodyguards. One evening, in a place called the Audubon Ballroom in New York, Malcolm X was assassinated while giving a speech. My father was forced to leave the New York metro area, and so we moved from New York back to Greensboro, North Carolina, and that is where I grew up."

Lee's childhood was rather stable after moving back to Greensboro. "For the first fifteen years, it was fairly normal. Christmas, Easter, celebrating birthdays, going to Grandma's house. We grew up in the sixties and the seventies, so we grew up in that era with a positive attitude about being black and proud. You know, black is beautiful. My father was the head of the house and my mother was a schoolteacher." Rouson's seemingly idyllic life soon came to an abrupt end when his parents separated and his father moved to Chicago to advance in his company, Dudley & Fuller Products, an African American-owned cosmetic company.

About that time, Rouson was on the road to becoming a locally well-known athlete. "So about three years go by, and all of a sudden I'm in high school and I'm like really famous," said Rouson. "I'm the big-time football player. At this point, my father comes back. In my mind as a young person, I'm thinking my mother and father are going to get back together. So he was always around back then, even though he had a house in a little town near Greensboro called Kernersville, North Carolina."

Although his parents never did get back together, Lee's father remained in his life as a solid influence. "My father taught me a lot of things," said Lee. "His motto was, 'I am not going to raise males; I'm going to raise men.'"

One particular incident with his father left Lee with a lifelong memory of how to handle tough situations and live with one's choices. His sister was cut from the Pop Warner cheerleading squad because she was black, and his father asked Lee to make a choice in response to the situation. Should he remain on the football team, or should he leave? Lee remembers his father saying that "they cut your sister from the squad because she is black. That's not right. You've got three days to make a choice, whether to stay or leave."

"It was a really difficult time for me, but that is how my father raised me—to make choices. So I made a choice. I told him that if I quit now, nothing was going to change in America. So my father said, 'Well, you made your choice and I am not going to come and see you play football on Saturdays.'" Lee's father did not go see Lee play again until the last game of the year. "My mother, my aunt, and other people in the community would come to see me play on Saturday morning," Lee said. "Now my sister wanted to see me play the last game, so my dad did see me play the last game of that year."

Lee's father was also somewhat famous himself. "His nickname was Big Rou," Lee remembered. "Big Rou was well known because of how he treated people. He'd find a way to engage people and to command respect. My father had that ability. I remember all the ballplayers for the Giants would all want to come up and talk to him. He had conversations and relationships with all kinds of guys—especially Bill Parcells, the former head coach of the Giants."

As for the greatest thing his father taught him, Lee remembers one in particular—understanding how to show love to a woman. "He said, 'Lee, a woman can't love a man.' He told me that God didn't make a woman to love a man, but a woman's love for a man was in response to that man's love for that woman. So even though I didn't understand what he was saying, and even though I didn't see him living out what he was saying, that was the greatest thing that he taught me. That was driven home to me powerfully because the day that I surrendered my life to Jesus Christ, it was because I realized that God loved me and I responded to that fact."

Lee attributes that lesson from his father as saving his marriage too. He would remind Lee when he saw him struggling with some of his relationships that it was his responsibility as a man to be the one who shows and initiates love.

Lee also credits his father as being a great leader, which made an impact on him. "My father was a great leader. People followed him, people wanted to be around him, people respected him. He made people smile. He helped so many young athletes get scholarships to junior colleges all over the country. He helped people all of the time. He was an amazing leader and an extremely compassionate and caring person. Big Rou made everybody feel like they were somebody."

THE STORY: THE RÉSUMÉ (BY JOE PELLEGRINO)

Many fathers don't necessarily show a lot of emotion, but demonstrate their love by their actions. Those actions can often take many directions, but they speak the same language to a child. In my case, one such incident spoke volumes to me about my father's way of encouraging and supporting me.

By my senior year of college at the University of Scranton in Scranton, Pennsylvania, I had had enough of school. I was not a good student, but I felt I knew enough to get by pretty well. I was bright and hardworking. So I decided to double up on classes in the fall session of my senior year so that I could gain enough credits to graduate early. On January 31, 1984, I accomplished my goal. The next day I made the one-and-a-half-hour drive to my home in Wayne, New Jersey.

When I arrived home there was nobody there. As I walked into the empty house, I heard the phone ringing. I answered it and the person on the other end asked to speak with Joe Pellegrino. I said I was he, and she proceeded to tell me she was from Witco Chemical Corporation and had my résumé. She asked if I would like to come in the next day for an interview. I said sure. As I hung up the phone, it occurred to me that I never prepared a résumé, much less sent one out.

Who could have done this for me? When my dad came home, I told him what had transpired earlier in the day. He quickly told me it was he who had prepared the résumé and was sending them out to various companies who placed help wanted ads in the daily newspaper. You see, my dad, John Pellegrino, was the personnel manager for Lever Brothers, so he had a good understanding of what companies where looking for and therefore created a résumé for me.

I went to the interview and got the job, which I started the day after. I went from a college kid on a Monday to a working stiff on a Thursday. My dad was not a "that a boy" kind of cheerleader. I don't remember him coming to many of my games or verbally cheering me on. But behind the scenes, this old-school man was building me up in a way that started me on my successful journey. It's the little things that add up to big things. We all need a John Pellegrino in our corner. Thanks, Dad.

THINK ABOUT THIS

Both Lee's father and my (Joe Pellegrino) father were people who could influence others, and both were leaders to their sons, teaching us important lessons along the way. But fathers are also husbands. It's one thing to lead your child, but it does not stop or even end there. A biblical character trait of a dad is to self-sacrificially serve your spouse. We hear a lot about absentee fathers these days, but not much about absentee husbands. Influence is great, but it starts at home.

It's important for men to not just be a dad that the son or daughter might emulate or enjoy being around, but it's also important to reflect the Ephesians 5:25 and 28 admonition: "Husbands, love your wives, just as Christ loved the church and gave himself up for her.... Husbands ought to love their wives as their own bodies."

Fortunately, both Lee's father and my father understood that their influence in their homes would make an impact on us, despite shortcomings in other areas of their lives. Their presence alone would carry influence to change situations.

THE QUESTION

Each of us can be a person of influence in someone's life. Whom can you influence in your circle of friends, coworkers, or family, and lead them toward a deeper relationship with God?

Sonny Franzese

THAT'S MY DAD!

THATSMYDADMOVEMENT.COM

6

MICHAEL FRANZESE

THE UNSHAKEABLE FATHER

BACK STORY

Michael Franzese grew up as the son of the notorious underboss of New York's violent and feared Colombo crime family. At the age of thirty-five, *Fortune Magazine* named him as number eighteen on its list of the Fifty Most Wealthy and Powerful Mafia Bosses, which was just five spots behind John Gotti. At his peak, Michael masterminded brilliant scams on the edge of the legitimate business world to earn millions in cash every week, quickly becoming the target of Manhattan's famed federal prosecutor, Rudy Giuliani, who came up empty-handed in his efforts to put Franzese behind bars.

While producing a movie, Michael met a Christian dancer

named Camille Garcia, who turned his world upside down. After falling in love and eventually marrying Cammy, Michael pled guilty to racketeering charges and accepted a ten-year prison sentence. He then vowed to do the unthinkable—walk away from the mob. To this day, Michael Franzese is the only high-ranking official of a major crime family to ever publicly walk away from the mob, refuse protective custody, and survive. He is now a motivational speaker who uses the compelling experiences of his former life to speak to church audiences, corporate executives, professional and student athletes, and at-risk youth.

THE INTERVIEW

When you talk about family with Brooklyn-born motivational speaker Michael Franzese, it takes on a different twist than what most people understand that experience to be in their lives. The "family" that Michael refers to is the one describing organized crime. "My father, John 'Sonny' Franzese, was the underboss of the Colombo family, one of the five organized crime families in New York," Michael matter-of-factly said. "Dad was a very high-profile individual, always under investigation, and a major target of law enforcement. So I grew up with that influence around all the time."

He went on to say, "As much as my dad tried to keep all of the outside influences out of the family environment, it certainly impacted us quite a bit." With all the uncertainly of that type of lifestyle, Michael remembers one constant in his life—his father really loved his family. "He really loved my mom. He was a great husband, and a great father to his children."

Michael's father had three children from a first marriage that ended in divorce, and he was left with the children as a result. So the Franzese household was a Brady Bunch–type arrangement that caused some problems in the house. "My mom was very young and she had to accept three children from the former marriage right away," recounted Michael. "That was a strain on the marriage and the relationship—but he treated us all very, very well."

Despite the seemingly difficult circumstances growing up in such a household, Michael remembers his father being extremely patient with him and his siblings. "He was very patient. He always took time to teach me about life. I think I learned some of my best qualities in life from him—to be a good listener, to control my tongue, not to be quick to judge or condemn people—qualities that have stayed with me and have been really helpful throughout my life."

Michael went on to say, "He certainly tried to instill the right values in us, always told me that education was important, told me how properly to treat women and children—I learned great things from my dad."

He emphasized that although his father was involved in organized crime, he did not want that type of life for Michael. He always stressed the importance of an education, and actually pushed Michael to become a doctor: "He tried to keep me out of that life. Believe it or not, early on, even though he had issues with the law, he taught me to respect the law—he said that it was really nonproductive not to obey the law. I really have to say that throughout my childhood my dad really tried to instill the right values in us."

Like many children, Michael looked up to his father as a hero. "He was my idol," Michael stated proudly. "Even though he was involved in an organization that wasn't socially acceptable, he certainly taught me the right things. I loved him, and he was supportive of me as a child growing up."

Michael lived a rather normal life in terms of enjoying what most young boys of his age in New York did, which was play sports. He describes himself as a jock while in high school, playing all three major sports—baseball, basketball, and football. He recounts a somewhat humorous incident when he was playing baseball once.

"We tell the story about my dad arriving at one of my baseball games. He'd always come late for some reason and pull right up to the field in a big Cadillac or Lincoln, and walk over to the stands with five or six guys dressed in suits. The umpire would take one look at him and never call a strike on me. We jokingly used to say that it was beneficial to have a dad in the mob when you play sports."

One would think that such high visibility of someone in the mob would negatively impact a young man. But Michael states that he did not feel that pressure, and that his father never seemed to bring that pressure home: "He had an amazing quality in the end," Michael said. "There were times when we'd walk out the door and law enforcement agents would be all around. He would walk by them like they were invisible, like they didn't even exist. He just carried on as if they weren't there. They had some confrontations, but he would really try to dismiss their presence."

Despite Michael's love for his father, he knew early on things were different in the Franzese household because of all the media attention his father received. "I heard about him in the schoolyard from kids," Michael remembers. "Also, we had a housekeeper at the time who was from England. Her name was Pauline and she actually told me a lot of stuff going on with my dad when I was younger. But I never heard it from him—he would never sit down and discuss any of it with me."

One thing that Michael enjoyed was going out with his father to famous restaurants and clubs. "I loved going to the Copacabana (the famous New York City nightclub) with him," Michael remembers. "We did that quite often, as he knew the owner. We saw some of the best talent in the world, from Sinatra to Sammy Davis Jr. Those were wonderful, wonderful times that I had with my dad, and we did it quite often.

"Also, when we got a bit older, we had a New Year's Eve tradition where the whole family got together in our house to bring in the New Year together. And right after that we all headed into Manhattan and had a blast until seven or eight in the morning at different places that Dad would take us to. I enjoyed just hanging out with him. He was fun to be around."

As he stated previously, Michael is quick to point out that he learned many good things from his father; advice that served him well later on in life. "Whether in business or negotiation or just in general, my father taught me to always keep my mouth shut and be a good listener. Listen carefully and then respond intelligently. Never condemn or judge anybody too quickly. Those things really stood up throughout my life."

Despite the generally perceived violence of organized crime, Michael remembers that his father taught him to respect women, which has been a key to his marriage of more than thirty years. "What my father taught me certainly has been a major influence in my marriage. I've been married for thirty years now, and she's kind of my princess. We have our issues, obviously, like everybody else, but I respect her and she has been a great influence in helping shape our marriage."

Michael's love for his father is evident, but he is also quick to admit the things he wished his father had done differently with him. He said, "Early on in life I really had no issues with my dad at all. Yes, later on in life I followed him into his bad lifestyle. But knowing what the lifestyle was about, my dad should have done everything in his power to keep me out of it. He is the reason that I got into it when he went to prison. I think that he kind of caved in when I wanted to help him out when he went to prison, and he agreed to help me get into the lifestyle. If I was in this position and it was my son, I would do everything in my power to keep him out of that life. I wouldn't allow it, and I think that's the major issue. Even though I don't blame my father, this was my decision and I could have said no. Ultimately, he shouldn't have encouraged it when I wanted to move forward."

Michael's father is still alive at the time of this writing, and at ninety-eight years old he is the oldest living inmate in the federal system. One of the strangest twists to Michael's relationship with his father occurred when Michael was attempting to leave the mob. Normally, if one attempts to leave the mob, that's a virtual death sentence. As a result, a hit was ordered on Michael and agreed to by his father.

"Until this day, my father denies it," Michael said. "But the FBI told me that a contract had been put out on me, and my father went along with it. He denies it, but I would expect him to deny it because one thing my dad always told me was never admit to anything—never . He is not admitting to it still, but I know him too well."

Even though Michael Franzese's father lived the life of a member of the mob, he still feels he had a healthy relationship with his father growing up. "Despite whatever a parent does in his life," Michael said, "a child really wants to find a way to love their father. My father gave me every which way to love him despite the lifestyle he was in. People ask me how I can still love my father in spite of how legendary he is for all these murders, and more. And I say, 'Well, he was my father, and he treated me like a great father would treat a son.' And so I want to find ways to love my dad. I think that's important for people to know. In my eyes, my dad was a great husband, a great father.

"Hopefully, people can understand that their parents may not be perfect, but if they do the right thing in their household and treat their families right, a child wants to love them. I think that's the message here."

THE STORY: MEETING YOGI (BY JOE BATTAGLIA)

Despite his father being who he was, Michael still desired to be with him and receive his approval, much like all children. And Michael wanted to love him too, for that is woven into the heart of every child. The unconditional love that looks beyond whoever your father may be or what he's done was especially telling coming from someone involved in organized crime. Yet it only reinforces that need in all children to have memories with their dads that they can pass along someday to their own children.

I remember one of the most memorable times with my father, who came from Italy as an immigrant, at sixteen years old in 1936, to escape the obvious soon-coming war that was brewing in Europe. He came to the New York area, settled in as a master shoemaker and shoe repair specialist. And he raised his family. He immediately became a fan of baseball. He rooted for the New York Yankees and their ballplayers of Italian descent, men like DiMaggio, Rizzuto, and Berra. I remember many a summer night lying on the living room floor with my dad listening to Yankees games on the radio before they were televised.

He took me to my first Yankees game in 1961 when I was just eleven, and I've been going to them ever since. Little did I envision that one day I would be involved in Baseball Chapel (an organization that holds chapel on Sunday prior to the games as a replacement for church services players would miss that day), and actually provide devotional messages to Yankees players in their clubhouse.

Well, from time to time, I'd invite my father to come with me to these opportunities and then we'd stay to watch the game. In my mind, there is nothing more American than a father and son watching a ball game, eating a hot dog, and coming home without a voice because it was lost somewhere between the first pitch and the last out.

After the service, we would hang around for a few minutes talking to some of the players who had questions. This one particular time I almost gasped when Yogi Berra walked into the room. Now you have to realize that for an immigrant shoemaker to be inside the Yankees clubhouse was itself beyond expectation, but to have one of his idols walk in and right up to us was like a scene out of the *Twilight Zone*. It was my most memorable moment with my dad. His eyes lit up, accompanied by the widest grin I ever saw on his face, before that time or ever after. It was like turning a kid loose in a candy shop and saying, *It's Halloween, so take whatever you want!*

That day, I had the pleasure of introducing my dad to Yogi Berra. I felt like this was payback for everything my father had ever done for me, which was considerable. My father and Yogi spoke to each other for a few minutes in Italian, shook hands, and my dad was on cloud nine. For a moment there, when I saw that childlike grin on my dad's face, I felt like I was the father. I still tear up when I remember that day and the look he had on his face. It's branded in my memory forever.

THINK ABOUT THIS

All of us want to experience a moment like that with our dad. Some of us are fortunate to have a memory like that, but there are many of us who have not. I (Joe Battaglia) understand where Michael Franzese is coming from when he speaks about loving to be with his father, despite what his father may or may not have done as a member of organized crime. I can totally relate. It's natural, and it speaks to the power of a father in his son's life.

In much the same way, God is a heavenly Father who wants to spend time with us. The extreme universal significance of the need for and role of a father in our lives is best expressed in Psalm 65:5, where it says that God Himself promises to be a father to the fatherless. God says He will actually step into a situation and assume a specific role for us—He will be our father. Like He has nothing else to do, right?

It is tragic when our society downplays or even mocks the role of fathers, for those who do so do not understand the significance God attributes to a father. In creating that role, God is actually painting a picture of Himself that He inserts into the context of the entity He established to give order to the universe—the family unit. A father is that important. Is there any wonder that we are hardwired to want to please our fathers, regardless of who they are or what they do?

THE QUESTION

Dad, you are your child's number one role model. That means your actions and words will inspire your child to either become like you or stay away from you. Knowing this, what changes will you make in your life today?

"People felt comfortable with Dad; they laughed with him," Berra's son Tim said. "Dad had a great way of relating to everyone. Sure, he was this iconic, great baseball player, but to me he was Dad. He was a buddy of mine. I wanted to be like him, a sensitive guy with an air of confidence and friendliness."[1]

Tim Berra reflects on his dad, Yogi Berra.

1 Ben Walker, "A wonderful life: Berra's family, Yankees honor Yogi," (Sept. 24, 2015), accessed Jan. 28, 2016, http://bigstory.ap.org/article/73268abae6dc45bfb368e82582557c79/wonderful-life-berra-family-reminisces-yogis-museum.

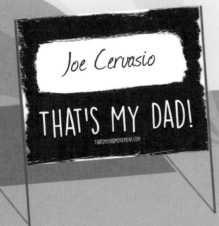

Joe Cervasio

THAT'S MY DAD!

THATSMYDADMOVEMENT.COM

7

TINA CERVASIO

THE FATHER AS FAMILY MAN

BACK STORY

Tina Cervasio is one of the most versatile sports broadcasters in New York. Currently, she's handling sports reporting and anchor duties on Fox 5 New York, hosting national talk radio on SiriusXM's NBA Radio, sideline reporting for Big Ten Network's College Football, and hosting New York Cosmos Soccer Broadcasts on ONE World Sports.

From 2006 to 2008, the University of Maryland graduate was the field reporter for the Boston Red Sox on the New England Sports Network (NESN), where she garnered multiple Emmy nominations and a personalized 2007 World Series ring. From 2008 to 2015, she won five New York Emmys for her courtside and feature reporting for MSG's Knicks game telecasts. She's also been a national sideline reporter for the NBA on TNT, the NFL on Fox, and a contributor on NBC Sports Network.

In addition to her television work, Cervasio has extensive experience in radio, including Olympics coverage, where she did play-by-play for women's hockey and gymnastics in Torino and Athens. Outside of sports broadcasting, Cervasio spends time with various charities, running the New York City Marathon in 2008, 2009, and 2013 to support the Garden of Dreams Foundation. She now resides in New Jersey with her husband, Kevin McKearney.

THE INTERVIEW

For seven years, Emmy Award-winning Tina Cervasio has worked for MSG covering the New York Knicks and Red Bulls soccer as a feature reporter and host, while also reporting and anchoring Fox 5 New York's *Good Day New York* and *Sports Extra*, and as a cohost on ESPN Radio, New York. Her love of sports and communication started as a child, and was nurtured by her father, Joe Cervasio, whom she feels is the best communicator in her family. That, according to her, is his best characteristic.

The Bellville, New Jersey, native was raised with her sister like many other Italian-American families—sharing traditions during the holidays, going to church on Sundays, and eating early dinners on Sundays of "macaroni and meatballs." Tina recalled, "We ate dinner together almost every night, except when my dad had to work late or was traveling. I remember, as a little girl, my sister and I would hear either the garage door opening or keys in the front door, and know Daddy was home. As the door finally opened, he'd whistle the same tune each time, and we'd run into his arms. You would think we hadn't seen him in months."

Tina's strong sense of family represents some of her fondest childhood memories, especially the pride her dad would feel when he'd take them to either a Belleville High School football game or a game at Cornell University, his two alma maters. "He didn't break every record, or was an All American, but he was All County," she said. "But the athletic and academic honors he earned afforded him to have a great education, a better future than his parents, shaping the person he is today, and gave him great stories to tell as a writer now later in his life."

As with siblings in most families, Tina and her sister have their own distinctive personalities. "My sister and I are very different. I have a passion and knowledge for sports and public speaking. And I'm emotional, expressive, and creative, which is a lot like my dad. My sister is analytical, brilliant in math and science, and business savvy—I am none of those.

"My father always praised our differences, embraced our personalities, and treated us exactly the same. To this day, he consults us on our careers, encourages us with our families and spiritual things. When my sister and I talk, many times we will say to each other, 'Well, Daddy told me to do this...or handle the situation like this...' And we always agree or use our father's advice, even if he gave it to the other daughter."

In the Cervasio household, her dad always said that her mom was the boss, which is how he communicated his respect for his wife. "That's my dad's rule," she said. "And maybe that's why my sister and I, as strong women, love him so much. My father always related that our mother was the CEO of our family. It's simple. She was the decision maker and leader, but also just as compassionate as she was a disciplinarian."

Tina learned firsthand how much her father treasured her mom every time they would go out. "They'd get dressed up and my father would always compliment my mother about how great she looked. He would even point out clothes or jewelry: 'Look at your mom, girls. Doesn't she look beautiful with those pearls?'

"I learned that this is the ultimate man—one who respects a woman and her natural personality traits as well. My mother is as hard a worker as anyone I know, a lifetime educator as a teacher, principal, and administrator, and my father both respected her determination and work ethic and supported her goals. He does the same with my sister and me too."

Being the sports enthusiast she is, Tina's idea of the perfect date with her dad was going to sporting events. She fondly remembers going to Friday night football, or a high school girls basketball game, or one of the local college football games at Columbia or Princeton. Ultimately, her career was shaped by these times with her father: "So many times, my mom was tired from working, or wanted to stay home to straighten the house, or was preparing for company the next day, so my dad would take me to a local sporting event. We would talk about the game, he would explain plays to me and answer my questions about the best players. I loved those times, just because they were fun—always exciting."

As she's already stated, she and her sister still seek their father's advice on a number of things. The best piece of advice she received from her dad was "staying in the moment" and "being in the now." Tina said, "It's both a fundamental way on approaching life and its challenges, but also comes from much of his biblical studies and our faith in God.

"Being such an energetic, expressive person that I am, at a young age my father started to instill in me about not getting emotionally too high or too low, and to never dwell in the past (especially about failures or shortcomings) or look too far in the future either, as that will cause unnecessary stress. It's a lesson of focus, which I believe comes from his discipline in sports and academics."

Joe's admonitions to his daughters were rooted in Psalm 23, which teaches surrender to God, and letting Him lead as the Shepherd. "He taught us to be still in one's actions, even in tough times (the valley of the shadow of death)," Tina recalled. "God will comfort you then, while preparing your future, where He will lead you down the right path (to where your 'cup runneth over'). So again, be in the moment, focus, be still, and surrender."

Staying in that moment has contributed to her success, Tina admitted. "I think my success today is based on me being persistent, resilient, but also honing in on 'that moment,' whether it's interviewing a superstar NBA player after he sets a franchise scoring record or just preparing for my broadcasts. When I have a soccer game, I prepare and focus on just that game. In those hours you need to prep—you don't worry about your NBA Radio show two days from now. Stay in the moment. I believe you can't bounce back from something negative if you keep looking back on it. So I focus on what I'm doing now to move forward."

Tina attributes much of her success in her personal relationships with friends and coworkers as a result of her father modeling this treatment of others for her and her sister. "The way my father treated my mother and the way he revered his late parents, and adores his friends, has no doubt influenced me to treat people as he did," she said. "I tend to always see the best in people, strive to be nice to everyone I meet, and I genuinely like everyone. Sometimes that is to my disadvantage, because I think everyone will like me back or treat me the same way—and then I must be willing to forgive."

The best thing about her father is that he has always been there for his daughters. "He is always there—always. He provided for my mother, sister, and me without abandon. Whenever I need him, he is a phone call away. Every dance recital, softball game, diving competition, football game when I was a cheerleader, track meet, award ceremony, each event I have been an emcee—and every single time I'm working on television or radio, he is there, watching me, supporting me—from when I was a little girl until now at age forty."

There is no doubt that Joe's ever present role as father, Tina readily admits rather proudly, has been an inspiration to her, which is something she hears from others about him as well, whether they are associates, former teammates, or people he has taught or consulted with. "They always use the same word—'inspiring,'" she said. "Whether it's from one of my father's speaking engagements, or how he treated his employees as a boss, or in his books he has written and published—it's about inspiring others, making them feel better about themselves in that moment, giving them new tools to use in life, and then moving forward to find more happiness, success, or the fulfillment they are looking for. He gets people going. He reenergizes them with the information he provides. As a result, he makes me want to inspire others. Even if his advice isn't perfect for the situation

I'm in, it still inspires me. That's his legacy to me and my family, and to so many others as well."

THE STORY: A WORLD SERIES VICTORY
(BY JOE PELLEGRINO)

With one swing of the bat, New York Yankees first baseman Tino Martinez changed the complexion of the entire 1998 World Series against the San Diego Padres. Clearly, this was one of the most exciting games the series has ever produced, and to have it occur in New York made it even bigger.

I have been a big Yankee fan since I was about ten. Quite frankly, the Yankees were the first thing I ever really locked onto. During a difficult childhood in which I had no self-esteem or self-confidence, baseball became my release and the Yankees became the object of my affection. After twenty-eight years, you can rest assured that my affection for the Bronx Bombers still burns strong. I still receive a tremendous amount of pleasure watching the team play and following their progress, especially the record-breaking seasons of the last five years. I have been fortunate to get to know many of the players through Baseball Chapel, an organization set up to bring church to the stadium on Sundays. I also got close to the baseball scene through coauthoring of a sports book entitled *Safe at Home*. In fact, I actually got to the point where I was rooting more for the guys I knew than for the other guys who were labeled superstars.

Since I have been a fan, the Yankees have been involved in eight World Series, including the magical season of 1998. I made a determination that year (1998) that the team was good enough to get to the Fall Classic, and I was going to make it a point to be there to cheer them on. To guarantee me a spot, I purchased a partial season ticket plan, which gave me two tickets for every Friday night game at the stadium. It also assured me of two seats for the first game of every playoff series, including the World Series. I attended the first two playoff series and had an incredible time. However, when it became apparent that the Yanks were headed to the World Series, my wife mentioned to me that our church was having a father-daughter dinner.

"Great," I replied. "When is it?"

She replied, "Saturday, October 17."

I immediately cringed, thinking that could be the first game of the series. The tickets did not have a date on them, so I called the Yankees and they confirmed my fear: the first game was on the seventeenth. I then asked the ticket sale representative if I could trade the first game for the second game of the series, and their reply was simple: "No exchanges. No returns."

I slumped. My dream of attending a World Series was now in serious jeopardy. What could I do? I called several ticket brokers and asked them if they would be interested in trading Saturday tickets for Sundays. They said no, but they would buy my tickets and sell me Sunday's tickets. That sounded really great. There was only one problem, however—they wanted double for the tickets than what they would pay me for my tickets—which was not an option.

The bottom line became clear: if I wanted to go to the series, I had to go on Saturday night. I prayed about it and knew the right thing to do. My daughter Jenny, who was six at the time, then asked me in that incredible way of hers whether or not we were going to the dinner. At the time she asked, I was reading the sports page and on the front of the paper was a big story on the Yankees with a picture of some of the players. After she asked, I told her something special was happening that night and I held up the paper and pointed to the picture. Her bright smile faded. She felt that I had chosen the game over her. I could only take about three seconds of her pain and then quickly smiled. Still pointing to the picture I said, "It is a very special night because it is going to be *our* night!" Her smile returned even bigger than before. She knew what I was giving up, and she knew exactly where she stood in my eyes. It is something she will never forget, nor will I.

I will never forget it because five minutes after we got to the dinner, Jenny asked me if we could leave. I calmly got down on one knee and, looking into her eyes, told her that we would be staying for the length of the dinner. And that is exactly what we did.

We arrived home just in time to see Tino hit that grand slam, and, you know, it was okay that I wasn't there. After all, I got my money back for the tickets (and yes, made a little extra coin), but, more importantly, my daughter knew that no game or meeting or anything else would ever be more important than her.

THINK ABOUT THIS

Priorities are always about choices. Tina Cervasio and Jenny are both thankful for the choices their fathers made that impacted them in a significant way. You can't put a price tag on those type of decisions. Neither a World Series ticket nor an Emmy come even close to the worth of hearing your father say, *I value time with you above these other things.*

In Mark 5:21–43, a father made a choice to seek out Jesus in order to impact his daughter. He was obviously a family man like Joe Cervasio. But Jairus had a more desperate need. His daughter lay dying and he did the only thing he could—seek out Jesus and believe that only He could save her life. He pleaded with Jesus and so He went with him to his home. Before they got to the house, however, Jairus' servants came out and informed him that his daughter had died.

Jesus calmed Jairus' fear, went into the house, and raised her from the dead. Imagine the feeling in his heart to see her snatched from death's door. What greater gift could any father be given, than to see his child restored to life? To all who will seek Him and believe, the heavenly Father offers to raise all His children from spiritual death. He is the ultimate family man.

THE QUESTION

Sit down and make a list of your priorities. Are there any changes needed to this list? If so, work toward putting those changes into practice.

Coaches Willie West
& Brooks Hurst

THAT'S MY DAD!

THATSMYDADMOVEMENT.COM

8

DARRYL STRAWBERRY

THE BROKEN FATHER

BACK STORY

Darryl Strawberry was one of the most feared home run hitters in baseball, earning nicknames such as Strawberry's Field Forever and the Legendary Straw Man. Born on March 12, 1962, in Los Angeles, Darryl was the number one overall pick in the 1980 amateur draft, and he quickly lived up to lofty expectations. He was twenty-one when he made his Big League debut in 1983 with the New York Mets, hitting twenty-six home runs to win the National League Rookie of the Year Award.

He enjoyed his finest season in 1987, hitting a team record of thirty-nine home runs and stealing thirty-six bases to join baseball's exclusive 30–30 club. He led the league with another thirty-nine homers and a .545 slugging percentage in 1988, earning a second-place finish for the National League's Most Valuable Player Award.

In 1995, after stints with the Dodgers and Giants, Strawberry joined the New York Yankees, where he starred in the 1996 and '99 playoffs for the Bronx Bombers. Strawberry finished his career with three 335 home runs, 1,000 RBIs, and eight All-Star selections. Today, Darryl's purpose and passion is serving the Lord Jesus Christ by speaking a message of hope, helping others transform their lives through the power of the gospel of Jesus Christ.

THE INTERVIEW

Darryl Strawberry achieved immediate fame as a rookie member of the New York Mets, and later with their crosstown rival, the New York Yankees. He was feared at the plate, but it was his own fear of his dysfunctional background that drove him to succeed as a professional athlete.

He was raised by what he describes as "a raging-alcoholic father." His home life was hostile and dysfunctional. "This type of environment damages a child deeply inside," Strawberry said. "I encourage all fathers to take your rightful place. If you need help and healing, then get it. If you are an absentee father, become present. If you do not know how to be the dad God created you to be, seek out a true man of God and allow him to guide you. We need to raise our children to be strong men and women of God through love, care, discipline, and honoring the Lord Jesus Christ."

Born and raised in Los Angeles, Strawberry is hard pressed to come up with a favorite childhood memory. Instead, he most remembers the physical abuse inflicted by his father, who beat Darryl and his brother, Ronnie. "He physically, mentally, and verbally abused my mother as well," Darryl recounted. "She was a beautiful woman, whom we all adored and loved, but were powerless over our situation as children. I learned violence. I learned how to become angry and enraged."

Darryl cannot remember a time he and his father did anything together, or any advice his father gave him. "I had to learn how to be a man on my own. My desperation to get myself out of that life was the driving force behind my success. I was determined to get out and become somebody."

Because of the way his dad treated him, he was determined to break the cycle of abuse in his own family. "I never laid my hands on my children. I broke the cycle of abuse. I allowed the Lord Jesus Christ to come into my life and change me from the inside out. I attached myself to men who were great examples of what a real man and father should be. My father was a man who did what was done to him—he repeated the cycle of abuse. I broke it. I have forgiven him and I pray for him."

Darryl emphasized how important it is to turn things around if you came from a dysfunctional family. "We need to become the fathers God created us to be, raising up strong, loving, successful, and God-fearing children who love the Lord and live according to His Word—especially in this world we live in today. I cannot stress the importance of the role of a father to his children."

THE STORY: WILLIE ALFONSO
(BY JOE BATTAGLIA)

Willie Alfonso grew up as one of seven children in the Williamsburg section of Brooklyn, New York, under the most horrible conditions imaginable. And yet he has become a pastor, motivational speaker, and chaplain to several New York professional sports teams. He describes his childhood as "horrifying" and a "nightmare." "My father was a straight-up alcoholic," Willie remembered. "He used to beat my mom almost every day, and the kids as well. My sister Yvonne and I got the worst of it, but he treated all of us the same. He would use these big iron spoons and garrison belt with ball bearings. He was just a brutal man."

Life was especially hard for his mom too. "My mom was a woman who just endured whatever he did. She wouldn't gather up the courage to walk away, so she kept us in that abusive life." To survive, Willie was forced to leave the house at age eleven due to an encounter with his father. "I was around eleven years old, and my father was beating my mother and I got the courage to hit him and get him off her."

As a result, Willie had to live in the streets, in abandoned buildings and store basements. Sometimes he'd find refuge with family members, like his uncle Frank. To eat, he'd often resort to stealing. Sometimes, he'd find a job and make a couple of bucks to buy food. During all that time, however, his father never came to look for him. "I was sixty-three years old when my father passed away. He never once told me he loved me."

To Willie, the greatest lesson he learned from his childhood experience was to simply survive. And being surrounded by all that violence made him prone to violence himself. He described himself as "a walking time bomb." He said, "You know, I was sniffing glue, smoking pot, doing heroin, and cocaine—just living a very destructive life."

Willie continued in that lifestyle until he was twenty-seven, when God stepped into his life and things began to change. "I was around twenty-seven, never went to school, so I didn't know how to read or write. But I wasn't stupid. If you taught me something, I would learn it. So I learned how to print on printing machines. I was working in a print shop and there were like sixty guys working there, all Blacks and Hispanics, and they hired a new supervisor. He was a white, blond-haired, blue-eyed German man named Otto Lange, and he was a Christian. The first thing he said to me was that Jesus loved me. My response to him was that was for them white people, and not for me. I thought, 'Where was your Jesus when I was eating out of a garbage can, and I was living in the street? That isn't for me, brother, that's for you.'

"But every single morning he'd share with me a Bible verse and tell me that Jesus loved me. At first, I was mean to him, like when I'd glue his Bible pages together and he couldn't open it. Once, he started a Bible study and a minute before Bible study I would light up two or three joints and smoke the room up. I did everything possible not to hear this guy talk."

And then one day, Willie could not get past the love and hand of God on his life. He knew very little about being a man, let alone being a husband. "I never had a role model to teach me. But I have been married for forty-three years now," he said.

In time, and with the help of his newfound faith, Willie began learning how to unpack the baggage. "It takes time," he emphatically stated, "and we all have one or two things that we struggle with deeply. We have to learn how to have a renewal of the mind and how to change those things."

Willie will often look back and marvel about how much different he is from his father. "I had to start getting a renewal of my mind and learning how to be a man, learning how to be a father, learning how to be a husband. You know, I had to learn how to be patient—all these things that were not in me. I am still learning them and am by far better than before, but I am still learning them. I believe that is why the Lord tells us we are to work out our salvation. It takes work."

THINK ABOUT THIS

Willie Alfonso and Darryl Strawberry both understood brokenness and the toll it takes on you, whether as a star athlete and celebrity or someone from the streets. The apostle Peter also understood it as well. He denied Jesus three times, turning his back on the one whom he swore he'd defend to the death just hours earlier. The resurrection saved Peter from a life of torment for what he'd done, just as the resurrection has saved Darryl and Willie from repeating the lives of their fathers.

The measure of a man working through brokenness understands that God looks for His people in the junkyards and pawnshops of life, and He offers top dollar for redeeming them from those messes. Many people today have lived through the brokenness of a father relationship and yearn to be restored, to hear the words *I love you* from their father. Tragically, however, they may never hear that from their earthly father. But God promises to be a "father to the fatherless."

Darryl and Willie have experienced that amidst terrible upbringings. They have found forgiveness from God so they could in turn forgive their fathers. Their brokenness did not end there, however. They were restored and have gone on to become fathers and family men. They too can now say about their heavenly Father, "That's my Dad."

THE QUESTION

God specializes in repairing and restoring broken lives. If there's anything in need of repair in your life, it's never too late or beyond repair. Go to God with your concerns and experience His love and forgiveness today. What is it in your life that you need God to repair today?

Burgess Harmon Richards

THAT'S MY DAD!

THATSMYDADMOVEMENT.COM

9

FRANCES HESSELBEIN

THE THOUGHTFUL FATHER

BACK STORY

Frances Hesselbein is one of the most highly respected experts in the field of contemporary leadership development. She is the president and CEO of the Frances Hesselbein Leadership Institute, which was originally founded as the Peter F. Drucker Foundation for Nonprofit Management, but renamed in 2012 to honor her legacy and ongoing contributions.

Mrs. Hesselbein was awarded the Presidential Medal of Freedom, the United States of America's highest civilian honor, by President Clinton in 1998 for her leadership as CEO of Girl Scouts of the USA from 1976–1990, as well as for her service as "a pioneer for women, volunteerism, diversity, and opportunity."

From 2009–2011, she served as the class of 1951 Chair for the Study of Leadership at the United States Military Academy at West Point, in the department of behavioral sciences and leadership, where she is the first woman, and the first non-graduate, to serve in this chair.

She has served on many nonprofit and private sector boards, including chairman of the National Board of Directors for Volunteers of America from 2002–2006. Mrs. Hesselbein is the recipient of twenty-one honorary doctoral degrees, and she is editor-in-chief of the award-winning quarterly journal *Leader to Leader* and is the coeditor of twenty-seven books in twenty-nine languages.

THE INTERVIEW

Frances Hesselbein has been one of the leading leadership gurus in the nation. As the founding president of Peter F. Drucker Foundation and former CEO of the Girl Scouts of the USA, she knows a lot about influence. The role of her dad in her life was highly influential, for he is the person whom she describes as the epitome of "loving thoughtfulness."

Frances was born in Johnstown, Pennsylvania, a little town amidst the mountains of western Pennsylvania, near Pittsburgh. She grew up in family of three, with a younger brother and sister. "I adored them," Frances stated. "I loved to take care of them."

The family lived in a redbrick house that Frances' father built for them, and they were only nine miles from Frances' grandparents, whom she adored as well. She remembers that her dad always treated her, her siblings, and her mom with great patience and kindness. "I never heard him raise his voice," she said. "Mother was just the opposite—not very calm. That's where I learned that when you love someone, you find ways to take care of them and bring out the best in them."

Her father worked in Pittsburgh during much of her childhood and wasn't actually around all that much. Frances still felt that when he was there, it was a wonderful, loving experience. She had a close relationship with her father and calls it "the most beautiful part of my growing up." What she fondly remembers most was listening to her history that dated back to the Second Lord Baltimore in the 1400s, who brought a ship loaded with people from Oxford County, Newgate Village, England. "They landed and called where they landed Baltimore," she said. "I think it was 1463. My father wrote down our history, so we have a wonderful family history to pass down to future generations. When we lost him when I was seventeen, I had these family stories already memorized."

Frances' father had been in the army in the Philippines during World War II and was exposed to a type of gas that eventually destroyed the aorta leading from his brain to his heart. "I was alone with him when he died," Frances recounted. "I remember stroking his forehead and saying to my father, 'Daddy, don't worry about John and Trudy, I'll take care of them.'"

Despite losing him early in her life, Frances learned much from her father—in particular, respect for all people. "These days," she said, "we observe so little respect in our world. We hear leaders speaking about one another in ways that at one time we would never do. We might say, 'Well, I do not agree with your position on this, but I respect it.' That is not today's world. My father communicated this message of respect in many, many ways. To this day, I'm so grateful."

Another important thing she learned from her father was the use of language. "He taught me to distill language until you used the fewest possible words to make the greatest impact," she said. "Later I distilled it further to describe what a leader has to be: mission focused, values based, and demographic driven, which means we manage for the mission or we are part of the past."

At the time of her father's death, Frances had recently enrolled at Johnstown Junior College. From there, she broke down barriers for women in what was always a man's world. The highlight of that career, she said, culminated as the CEO of the National Organization of Girl Scouts of the USA. "For thirteen years," Frances said, "I never had a bad day. I had some tough ones, but never had a bad day."

Frances is quick to acknowledge that her father's legacy was leaving her with a passion for the historical birth of our country. "I love my country and I love the history of it, and the role my family played in its history," Frances proudly stated. "John Adams was one of my ancestors and the only founding father who never owned a slave. I watched the respect my father had for the history of our family and those who lived before us and shared in every war beginning with the Revolution, to the War of 1812, to six brothers fighting in the Civil War. To this day, my son is a soldier and my brother and my husband all served."

Then she reiterated, "As I said, the words that best describe my father are love of country, and he helped me understand that this was a great privilege."

THE STORY: THE GREETING (BY JOE PELLEGRINO)

Dave Swanson was a great man, friend, and mentor. He was the executive director for Baseball Chapel, which, through the blessing of Major League Baseball, arranges church services every Sunday to the Major and Minor League Baseball teams throughout the country. Dave taught me many lessons, but there is one in particular that sticks out.

Each Sunday Dave would go to either Yankee or Shea Stadium to oversee the chapel for that day. Several times I tagged along with him as he was seeking to involve me more in the organization. Each time I went with him, I noted that Dave would greet each person he saw along the way to the locker room—and he did this consistently. It was obvious the people respected him and enjoyed his jovial greeting.

But there was one instance that left an impression on me. Each time we went, there was a well-known sportswriter Dave would always say hello to. But the sportswriter never reciprocated. This one day we were in the locker room and Dave passed the sportswriter, but being somewhat preoccupied he did not greet him. The sportswriter grabbed Dave's arm and said, "Hey, where is my hello?" I guess we all like to be thought of, even if we don't acknowledge it at times.

THINK ABOUT THIS

There's something special about people who are always thinking about others. Their thoughtfulness is refreshing. In fact, thoughtfulness considers others, and their respective situations, and makes no distinction whether a response is received because it's not about what one receives. Frances' father and Dave Swanson were two such people.

Joseph, the father of Jesus, also exemplified that quality in a more remarkable way. His thoughtfulness extended way beyond the normal consideration that would be given in the first century. When he found out that his betrothed Mary was pregnant, his thoughtfulness took on a supernatural significance.

The acceptable response for his culture and custom was to have Mary stoned at worst, or to simply walk away at best. Either decision was not an easy one when directed toward the one you love. Yet Joseph's thoughtfulness played a key role in the birth of Christ. He could have walked away, but chose not to. And, in doing so, he kept the family together. He considered Mary's situation, and I believe his heart was prepared to receive the angel's direction for his life.

We often lack thoughtfulness and so God cannot enter into our situation. Thoughtfulness opens the door for spiritual solutions, it fosters an environment in our heart to hear from God, and it also changes the course of history. If we are to be fathers who leave a lasting impact on our children and grandchildren, then we must be thoughtful people, passing that character trait on to future generations.

THE QUESTION

In what area of your life can you extend thoughtfulness to another individual and open a spiritual door that will impact others in a positive way?

Jesse Tyree

THAT'S MY DAD!

THATSMYDADMOVEMENT.COM

10

DAVID TYREE

THE JOYOUS FATHER

BACK STORY

David Tyree etched himself in New York City folklore, as well as in NFL history, by making what many consider to be the greatest catch in Super Bowl history, when he pinned the football on the top of his helmet, enabling the Giants to score the go-ahead touchdown with 39 seconds left in the game. At the end of the day, all he could do was give glory to God, thus honoring his Savior Jesus Christ.

Drafted in sixth round of the 2003 NFL draft by the New York Giants (211 overall), Tyree ended up being named to *Pro Football Weekly*'s All Rookie team as a special team's player and one of the few Giant rookie receivers in recent years to record a hundred-yard receiving performance.

Along with his professional achievements on the field, David has a personal desire to see others experience the fullness of God's love. Today, David and his beautiful wife, Leilah, sit on the board of Children of the City, which is an organization that has successfully served the children and families of southwest Brooklyn for more than two decades by changing the culture of poverty through education and outreach.

THE INTERVIEW

David Tyree will always be known for his third-down "helmet catch" in Super Bowl XLII that enabled the New York Giants to march downfield in their final drive to score the winning touchdown against the New England Patriots. It's been called one of the greatest receptions in football history. But if you ask David Tyree what he feels may be the most important catch in his life, he'd say that would be inviting Jesus Christ into his life.

David's childhood was marred by his parents' divorce when he was just two years old. So he remembers very little about his relationship with his father, even though he stayed in the same town as David throughout much of his life. But David did remember one thing about his father—he was joyful. "In one word, my dad was always one to bring joy. He was a quite a character. My mom took care of business, and my dad was involved in as much as he could be while not being at our home."

David grew up in East Orange, New Jersey, as a youngster, and then moved to St. Thomas for a few months when he was ten, which was challenging for his dad, David recalled. After a few months in St. Thomas, his family moved back to Montclair, New Jersey, a neighboring town of East Orange. "It was a change of pace, better education, and my dad was still close by in East Orange," David remembered. "I had a fairly good upbringing."

Even though his father was not living with the family, he'd always encourage David toward an education. "He always encouraged us to get an education and was a major support of my involvement in sports. He was a super proud father. He was considerate, he cared, and he did his best considering the situation. There was never a time I felt abandoned by my dad because he did not live with us. And he never would put me in a position to disrespect or dishonor my mother."

One incident in particular stands out to David that exemplified that position. "I had a fallout with my mom, and I walked from Montclair to Orange to my dad's house (to let some steam out), which was a few miles away," David recalled. "I told him what happened, and he set me straight. He told me, 'You know what you did was wrong, and you need to get yourself together. Take the time to get it together, but you need to get back home.' He never created the opportunities to allow me to dishonor my mom."

David is quick to acknowledge that his father had many admirable qualities, mainly respect for his mom, the importance of education, and an overall joy for living. "I think the biggest challenge for my dad," David feels, "was the lack of presence to exhibit those qualities in his home. That seemed to be a challenge he couldn't overcome."

David can't really remember ever getting advice from his father because most of what he learned was just in passing.

Despite the lack of guidance, however, David claims that his father was always positive. David said, "His sense of optimism and endurance was lived out when adversity came. He followed through more so by example than by advice. So, like my dad, my overall outlook on life is just pure optimism and endurance as well."

Because of his father's personal conflict over being divorced, David says that he grew up with a fear of failure. "Before I knew Christ, I grew up with the fear of failure, particularly so when my wife and I had our first son and we weren't together. That was a fear of mine—to have a son and be separated, like my parents were. By the grace of God, my life changed and we were reunited.

"I definitely had some elements in my life that I did not want to mirror after my father, but most of that became a by-product of being my father's son. I sort of became my father with my struggles with alcohol. My dad drank around me, so we drank together. My dad let me taste a sip of beer when I was a little kid, which set the stage for destructive patterns later on in my life. I saw those generational challenges coming into play.

"Fortunately, because my father was super proud of me and of my accomplishments in the world, he was eager to share the things he did right, like exuding confidence, and the continual encouragement of education. For me, those are more or less the patterns of behavior I want to give my children. I also realize that the one thing that matters is eternal life, and I want to raise them with that awareness and lay a foundation of godliness for them.

"Ultimately, my dad was a lover," David said. "He lived for his family. He's just an awesome man, and one I'm endeavoring to continue to honor, esteem, and pray for. Ultimately, the only thing he lacks now is Christ."

THE STORY: THE PIRATE SHIP (BY JOE PELLEGRINO)

When my son Joey was around eight, I would take him in the backyard and teach him how to play baseball. The deal was that if he hit the ball over my head, I would buy him a big LEGO pirate ship, which he really wanted. Unfortunately, he never hit the ball over my head. Or did he?

My son thought he did. But I disagreed. Regardless, it obviously bothered him because he thought that I reneged on the deal. When Joey was twenty-four years old, he took a job in the Orlando area. So in November 2013 we drove from New Jersey to Jacksonville, Florida, in record time. During our time in the car we had several conversations, mostly good. But there were a few that told me there still existed some tension between us.

Once we arrived we needed to get him settled in his new apartment, so our first stop was at the local Walmart. As we shopped for cleaning supplies and various odds and ends, I came across the LEGO aisle. As I stood in front of the new version of the LEGO pirate ship, I realized that ship was creating a wedge between us. And so I decided that it was time I did something about it. When I flew home the very next day, my first stop was Walmart, where I purchased that pirate ship, wrapped it up, and waited for Christmas.

When Joey came home for Christmas, I could not wait to give him this special gift. After all the gifts were given out, I told Joey I had one more for him, but before he opened it he needed to first read the card I had written for him. It said simply:

Joey,

This is long overdue, and for that I am sorry. Please accept this, late as it may be, for the continual home runs you are hitting in your life.

Love, Dad

The look on his face told the story. After reading the note, he said he knew exactly what the gift was. That day we spent Christmas at my brother-in-law Timmy's house. When Timmy asked Joey what he got for Christmas, Joey put his arm around me and said to Timmy, "My dad never has to buy me another gift." That meant the world to me.

No matter how bad you screw up, no matter how many years have passed, you can always do something about your past mistakes. Even if the person you go back to fails to forgive you, you will be released. I am so thankful that I tried to right a wrong, and I believe that Joey and I are better for it. It's never too late to right a wrong that was done in the past.

THINK ABOUT THIS

Dads don't always get it right. David Tyree's father tried his best to help his son despite the divorce, and I (Joe Pellegrino) realized that there was still one thing I needed to do to heal something between me and my son. And one of the greatest leaders of all time, King David, really blew it with his son as well.

The common theme throughout these relationships and throughout Scripture is redemption. It's never too late to right a wrong with someone, or right yourself with God through what

Jesus has done for us through His death and resurrection. The ultimate separation was God turning His face from His Son when Jesus became sin on our behalf (2 Corinthians 5:21)—that was a separation far greater and more painful than what any earthly father may have forgotten to do or say to his son.

Earthly fathers will falter, but our heavenly Father cannot falter or fail. The joy that David Tyree spoke of that his father brought into a relationship can never match the joy given by our heavenly Father. That joy, says Nehemiah, is the strength of our lives (Nehemiah 8:10). Fathers, if you are estranged from your sons and daughters today, God can help restore that relationship. He did it through His Son Jesus. Yes, the price was great, but the reward is even greater.

THE QUESTION

What do you need to do today to bring joy into your child's life?

Roderick Caesar, Sr.

THAT'S MY DAD!

THATSMYDADMOVEMENT.COM

11

RODERICK CAESAR

THE HONORABLE FATHER

BACK STORY

Dr. Roderick R. Caesar is the senior pastor of Bethel Gospel Tabernacle, being the son of its founders, Bishop Roderick R. Caesar Sr. and Gertrude Caesar. He received undergraduate and graduate degrees from Northgate Bible, Logos Bible, and Zion Bible Colleges. In 1994, however, Dr. Caesar was consecrated to the office of bishop and became the overseer of Bethel Gospel Tabernacle Fellowship; it was at this time that he also had conferred upon him an earned doctorate from Vision Christian College. Dr. Caesar shepherds congregations of several thousand members, and he is also the overseer of branch churches, including a thriving church in Haiti. He lives in Hollis, Queens, New York, with his wife, Beverly, and their four children.

THE INTERVIEW

Pastor Rod Caesar of Bethel Gospel Tabernacle in Queens, New York, is one of the most respected pastors in the New York metropolitan area, and nationally as well. Several years ago, he succeeded his father, Bishop Roderick Caesar, who served his church for over fifty years. Rod can only use one word to describe his father—that is the word *honorable*. "My father was true to his word in everything he spoke and everything he said," Rod proudly stated. "He was absolutely consistent. He was a man of honor, a man of integrity, and a man of his word. And he never deviated from that through all of the years that I was blessed to have him as a father."

Growing up in the Caesar household was a lot of fun for Rod. He said, "We knew for sure there was genuine love. It wasn't always articulated, but it was demonstrated through the level of commitment and dedication that he shared with us as a father. It was definitely very exciting. It was just my sister and me, and he was consistent with both of us. He didn't play favorites. What he would do for one, he would do for all. He was a nurturer, he shared his wisdom, and he gave us the best that he had to offer."

How his father treated him and his sister has carried over into how Roderick treats his children today. Rod stated, "What he showed me and what he taught me is what I have communicated to my children. A good example would be that the month of August every year was always family month. My father took off the month from church and shared that time with his wife, who is my mother, and with my sister and me. He treated my mom with the greatest sensitivity and care. He loved her.

"He loved her dearly and he demonstrated it in every way that I can imagine. So when I got married and started my family,

I did the same thing. The past thirty years or so, August has been a family month for me as well. I don't do anything in August other than spend quality time with my family."

His father's commitment to his family, though, did not come at the expense of his father's love for the gospel. "He was the kind of person who did not allow even his family to cause him to miss or to compromise on what his commitments were toward the things of God. The best demonstration for that would be on Sunday mornings. He would give us a sign-off on when he would be leaving for church. He would start, let's say, at ten thirty, and he'd say, 'I'll be leaving in fifteen minutes.' And then at ten thirty-five, 'I'll be leaving in ten minutes.' And at ten forty, he would say, 'I'm leaving in five minutes.' And then at ten forty-five, he'd say, 'I'll see you at church.'

"If we were not ready at ten forty-five, he would leave because no one was going to make him miss church or be late. My mother's name was Gertrude. He'd say, 'Gert, I'll see you at church.' She would say, 'I need five more minutes,' and he would say, 'I have to send someone for you. I have to be at church.' And he'd leave. He was totally, absolutely dedicated and committed to what his church was. She knew it and she never allowed it to be a stumbling block in their relationship."

Watching his father care for his mother influenced young Rod to care for his wife in much the same way. "I've always sought comfort in my wife's welfare above my own. If I have two dollars and she needs it for something, I would always defer to her and make sure that she is provided for first in every way."

Rod fondly remembers what he enjoyed most doing with his father, and what he learned from being with him. "What I really enjoyed doing with him was sitting at his feet and allowing him to just speak to me and share with me his life experiences and his wisdom. He was a wise man. I'm not into sports because my father was not into sports. Sports talk was not something we engaged in in our home. We were always in discussion.

One thing he learned, in particular, was to use time wisely. "My father always carried books with him wherever he traveled, wherever he went. When he went shopping with my mother, he'd stay in the car and read. He'd be researching or doing something. I picked up that habit from my father. I'm always engaged in something. I don't engage much in frivolity. I call much of what people watch on television today 'intellectual graffiti' because at the end of the afternoon you've watched a lot of television but you have benefited in no way from it."

That discipline he learned from his father has carried over into Rod's life as well. "I try to benefit from most of what I do. It is okay to laugh and to have fun. But every moment of your day, when you have nothing to do, you shouldn't be involved in just laughing and having fun. There should be some learning component to much of what we do in life."

The emphasis on learning and using time wisely did much to contribute to Rod's personal growth. He calls himself a lifelong learner. "I've always been a person who wants to know things. I mean, as a youngster, when I had free time, I used to read the dictionary. I carried a dictionary with me. It helped me tremendously. It increased my vocabulary; it gave me a great understanding not only of the English language but the culture in which I live. And I got that from my father. He wasn't a dictionary reader, but he had a phenomenal vocabulary. He was an excellent speaker. He had a phenomenal way of expressing himself. I learned that from him. That's one thing that he taught me."

And what was the best advice his father ever gave to him? Rod rattles off a number of things: "Stay true to what you know to be right. Stay true to God. Stay true to His Word. Be your own man. Don't follow the crowd—things of that nature. He constantly told me how important it was not to allow people to shape my values, but to shape them based upon what I know to be true from the Word of God. Let the Word of God be the standard."

That wisdom from his father has shaped Rod into the man and pastor he is today. "When I began in ministry, his best advice was that I should stay on the main highway. What he meant, of course, was don't allow other teachings, philosophies, and ideologies become the standard that you use to establish your own convictions. You know what truth is. Stay in the truth and let other people formulate their position. In this way, the thing that would be constant is that I would be making progress while others are redefining themselves and trying to find a new position. That was good counsel; that was good wisdom."

Still, Rod is a different man than his father. "What did I do differently? I'm a little more casual, more relaxed. Also, all my life Father always wore a black suit, a white shirt, a black tie, white socks, and black shoes. He always drove a black car. He was absolutely consistent. When he would go to buy a car, he'd say, 'What should I get?' because he knew I was into cars. So I would tell him what car to get, what color, and what options. He'd say okay, but when he came back from the dealership, it was a black car."

Rod relates a funny story of this consistency after his mother died and his father remarried. "I went to a convention where my father was as well, and I saw a man in a gray suit who very strongly resembled my father. I could not believe how close this man resembled my father in his general physical appearance. We were across a big room and I could not see his face." He continued, "Well, it was my father. Seems like when he got married again, his wife talked him into buying a gray suit. I was just absolutely shocked that my father would break from his tradition and not wear a black suit."

It was that consistency played out in his father's passionate love for God. "He honored God's Word in every imaginable way," Rod said. "There was never a question or doubt in any way. He always erred on the side of right."

Rod recalled an incident that really spoke to him about how his father trusted God to do what he felt God wanted him to do. "There was a man who came to my father once and requested assistance to help his family out of financial distress. There was something about the man that didn't read true with me. I felt like the man was a con artist, so I told my father not to help him. Nevertheless, my father proceeded to assist him. I said, 'Dad, when this man gives us such obvious indications of his lack of sincerity, why would you help him?' He just said, 'Well, it's not your money, so don't worry about it.' So I said to him again, 'Dad, I don't want you to loan this man the money because I don't think he's honest.' And again he said, 'Whatever the problem, it's between this man and me and God. You have nothing to do with it. If this man is not honest, if he takes the money, God will honor me because I'm giving with the right motive and God with deal with him because he's stealing the money.' With that thought in mind, he loaned the man the money. The man left town and never paid back his debt.

"So I went to my father and said, 'What do you say about this now?' He said, 'Well, as I said to you, I didn't do anything that I could not afford to do.' Then he asked me, 'Did I take any food from our dinner table? Have I denied you anything that you needed because I gave the money to someone else?' Of course to each question I had to say no, so he said, 'Then I have not lost anything, and neither have you. This man lost because he stole from a person who gave with the right motive and the right heart and the right intention. God will reward me and reward this family, and we will lack for nothing.' And that was it. That was his attitude. That was his posture in the situation."

Rod continued, "A life lesson he taught me was to never loan what you cannot afford to lose. He told me that loaning money makes enemies out of friends and it separates family. So he said, 'Don't loan money.' He told me to give money, and if people want to pay you back, then give them the privilege to do so. But do not loan money because loaning money will make an enemy out of a friend. And if you can't afford to lose it, then to give it to someone else would be foolish on your part. So make sure whenever you make that decision that it's something that you can learn to live without if you never get it back. And that's how I live my life to this day.

"When I loan people money, I allocate money to an individual to help them in a situation, and I do not think about it again. I do not let it obsess me in any way. If the person never pays me back, I have nothing to say. When I loan, I loan with the right motive, the right heart, and I don't charge any usury of any kind.

"If somebody needs a thousand dollars, to get a thousand dollars is all I expect back from them. If they promise to pay back, it's a thousand dollars—not a penny more. If they don't give it back, I made sure, just like my father said, it's not money that I needed for something else. If they don't pay me back, I'm still ahead of the game. It has benefited me tremendously throughout my lifetime."

Rod is quick to point out that his father's legacy is his love for the Word of God, the ways of God, the lifestyle of a believer, and emulating those pathways in life. "My father said to me, 'I will not leave you wealth, but I will leave you something that money can't buy. I'm going to give you a good name. If you hold to that good name, it will open doors that money won't buy. The name that I'm going to leave you with will have honor connected to it and it will be worth more than money.' He was true to his word. He left me with a name that has done for me more than any amount of money could never do."

Rod was right. The Caesar name carries a tremendous degree of respect and honor not just in the church community around New York, but in the church community both nationally and internationally. "I've gone to different countries and introduced myself," Rod said, "and the name has a level of renown that it has opened doors and made a way for me that I couldn't have made for myself."

THE STORY: TEACHING MY SON TO LIE
(BY JOE PELLEGRINO)

Early in my parenting life, I had a chance to see my lying transferred to my son. My wife and I took our small children to Hershey Park in Pennsylvania. Joey was three years old, and Jennifer was about a year old. Our funds were low, so I paid attention to a sign that said kids two and younger didn't have to pay admission. As we got close to the gate, I picked up my son and whispered in his little ear, "If they ask you how old you are, say you are two." I carried him to add to the illusion. Sure enough, he got in free and it was a great day at the park.

Do you remember how we said that in stressful situations we resort to our default persona? Standing in line at the park, I was stressed. I was wrestling with the shame that I didn't have a lot of money. As men, we often feel that money is power, and when we lack money we feel powerless. When I felt like I didn't measure up financially, I went to my default persona, which was a frequent liar. Without even knowing it, I was building that kind of default legacy for Joey.

On the way home, we stopped on the New Jersey turnpike for a burger. My son, who was incredibly cute and talkative, began chatting with the people in the next booth. The lady sitting there asked how old he was. I'll never forget his answer. He said, "Well, I'm three years old, but when I go to Hershey Park, I'm two." Man, did I feel like a worm.

Proverbs 14:12 says, "There is a way that seems right to a man, but its end is the way of death." You see, telling my son to lie "seemed right" while I was in line. "It's only a little lie," was the popular phrase running through my head, as was the reality that my wallet was light. In the end, the money I saved wasn't worth it. Something in me died when I realized that I had used my son and taught him to lie to save a few dollars. But my sin and my mistake taught me something too. I had an impure character that needed to be disinfected by the gospel of Jesus Christ. There was a lying side of me that needed to be buried.

I had a choice to make that day: Would my legacy to Joey be the impure example of a habitual liar, or the pure example of a godly man who honored truth? The change had to begin in me. Thank God that He didn't give up on me that day. Even though I knew I needed to change, it wasn't until Jesus empowered me that I really changed. I've learned that if God does something for someone else, then He can do it for me too. And you can be confident that if He did it for me, then He can also do it for you!

THINK ABOUT THIS

Honor is a word that seems to have lost a lot of meaning in our culture of self-gratification. You see, honor only has meaning if we have a view of something beyond and outside of ourselves. One of the Ten Commandments is "Honor you father and mother." Often, the way we learn that is to see our fathers and mothers acting honorably themselves.

Rod Caesar saw that daily fleshed out in his father's life and words. He understood the biblical maxim that "a good name is to be worth more than silver and gold" (Proverbs 22:1). That is the honorable man's "capital," the stuff he can take to the bank. It not only opens doors, but it opens hearts as well. Through honorable action, God steps in and bestows favor upon whatever the honorable man will touch. Fortunately, I (Joe Pellegrino) saw early on that for my son to honor me one day, I'd have to do the honorable thing and confess how I taught my son to lie.

Lies, like all sins, have no degree of gravity. One is not worth more than the other in the sight of God. The reason for this is that white lies often lead to the slippery slope of habitual lying. Like gateway drugs, you never know how addicted you can become to much harder drugs. The entry point to anything, whether bad or good, is the first step in that direction.

Today, if you're a father who has begun walking down that road of dishonor, it's not too late to turn around. Your children are watching you, and they are a lot smarter than you think. Your children truly do want to honor you, despite the fact that our culture will be telling them to do just the opposite. So make it easier for them to do so by showing them what true honor looks like.

THE QUESTION

Whom do you need to honor today that God has put into your life? What do you need to do today to restore honor to your name?

Edward Broussard

THAT'S MY DAD!

THATSMYDADMOVEMENT.COM

12

CHRIS BROUSSARD

THE FATHER AS AUTHORITY

BACK STORY

Chris Broussard is an internationally known NBA analyst for the ABC and ESPN television networks, as well as an award-winning journalist for *ESPN The Magazine* and ESPN.com. Broussard has costarred on the *KIA NBA Countdown Show* with basketball legend Magic Johnson and makes regular appearances on ESPN's flagship show, *SportsCenter*. He is also a consistent presence on *Outside the Lines, First Take, His & Hers, NBA Coast to Coast, SportsNation,* and *Mike and Mike in the Morning.*

A 1990 graduate of Oberlin College, where he earned a bachelor's degree in English, Broussard worked for six years as a reporter for *The New York Times*. While there he interviewed some of the world's most influential figures, including former president Bill Clinton and the Reverend Jesse Jackson. His achievements have led to his being listed among the 100 Black History Makers of 2012 by Thegrio.com.

In addition to his work as a journalist, Broussard is the founder and president of the K.I.N.G. Movement, a national Christian Men's organization. He is a spokesperson for former NBA star Allan Houston's Father Knows Best program, and he serves as a board member of Write-On Sports, a sports journalism program for teenagers; Athletes in Action, which is an international Christian sports ministry; and the New Canaan Society, which is a national Christian men's group.

THE INTERVIEW

When it comes to basketball analysts, none is better than ESPN's Chris Broussard, who covers the NBA with his own brand of insight that has made him one of the standout analysts in the game today. When he's not on-air, Chris is writing his regular columns for ESPN.com and *ESPN The Magazine*.

Broussard was born in Baton Rouge, Louisiana, but has lived in many different cities as a result of his father's work with Travelers Insurance Company. Chris' family was Catholic, so Sunday church was the norm. Eventually the family landed in Cleveland, Ohio, where Chris finished high school and attended Oberlin College, which was about forty minutes from Cleveland. His first job out of college was with the *Cleveland Plain Dealer* newspaper.

By his own definition, his father would best be described

as an authoritarian—with love. "He taught me how to respect authority," Chris stated, "his own authority first and foremost through discipline. We got spanked quite a bit, but it taught me how to respect my father's authority, and really, to be honest, that kept me in line. It kept me from drug use; it kept me doing well in school and knowing the importance of getting good grades and doing well, which obviously benefited me throughout my career. It also translated into respect for others who were in authority. I've never been a person who had any problem respecting authority, whether it was a pastor, a professor, or a coach. That benefited me in life, particularly on the job with editors. So when I think of how to best describe my father, authority comes to mind."

Chris describes his family as being tight-knit. "Our family was close, because, when you move a lot, initially all you have is each other. When you first go to a new city, you don't know anybody, so all you have are each other. I think that made our family close.

"My mother worked off and on when we were kids, although my father didn't want her to work. That's how he grew up. But as we got a little bit older, she began to work for the school board and ultimately ended up having a career with the school board. My mother cooked dinner pretty much every night. For the most part, we ate dinner together as a family every night. My father was definitely the person who ran the household though. We got spankings with discipline. My father has definitely pulled out the belt on many occasions. I have a brother who's a year younger than me and we're close now, but we also fought a lot when we were younger. In fact, 95 percent of the discipline I received was probably for fighting with my brother—not out of hatred. We just fought, you know, as siblings."

Chris and his brother might have fought about a number of things, but education was not one of them. "Education and hard work were emphasized—it wasn't a choice of whether or not we were going to be good students," Chris said. "We were both good students and that was that. We had to study and do well in school.

"Also, sports were a huge factor in our lives too. My father was a huge sports fan. Both my brother and I played football, basketball, and baseball growing up. I played all three sports through high school. Everything was about sports, like watching games, going to games, and watching my father play sports. Most of my father's interaction with us outside of just being a father was probably sports related. He coached us in basketball, baseball, and even football to some degree. I used to mess with him and say he was like Rollie Massimino, the coach for Villanova, because he was volatile and sometimes went overboard. He was hard driving, and he would yell at the referees. He definitely went overboard sometimes."

Chris' hard-driving, disciplinarian father would soften around his mother though. "He treated my mom well," said Chris. "They'd have arguments, but I think they've had a good relationship. They just celebrated their fiftieth wedding anniversary. I think sometimes they both talk to one another with more of an attitude than I think they should, but they have both been committed to each other and love each other.

"Everything was very family oriented. It's interesting when I hear some people talk about us being a close family—I never even thought about that as a kid. It was just like, 'This is my family—good, bad, or whatever—this is my family and we're close.' I certainly never thought we weren't close even when there were times when I was mad at my parents, when I was upset with them. But I never thought we weren't a close family or that I didn't love my family. Thoughts like that didn't enter my mind, as this was my family. We love each other and I never even considered if we were close or not. It was very good for me."

With the emphasis on sports in the Broussard household, it's no surprise that the thing Chris remembers most doing with his father were sports oriented. "What I probably most enjoyed with my father was throwing the football. When we played football, my dad was great at it. My brother and I would run post patterns and dad was the quarterback. Playing basketball with him was also fun. And we'd box when we were little too. He would come into the room and he would get on his knees and we would box with these boxing gloves we had. All these memories were fun. But I would say probably the most fun was when we threw the football, because football was my favorite sport and he was really into teaching us.

"When we were little, like eight years old, every Saturday my brother and I would go see my father play basketball with his friends at a high school in Cincinnati. Those were just great memories because your dad is your hero. I knew my dad wasn't perfect, and I saw his flaws. I think for most of his adult life, he's been a controlled alcoholic. I say he is controlled because he never got a DWI, and it never impacted his ability to work or his job performance. He drank and so did all my uncles and my grandparents, so drinking was a big part of our family. Thankfully, the drinking didn't hinder his career or his ability to provide for his family or encounter any problems with the law. But one thing it hurt was the quality of life in his relationship with my mother. Again, they have a good relationship, but it would have been better if he didn't drink. I know it bothered her at times."

With all the discipline his father expected from his children, Chris cannot recall a time when his dad sat down and gave them any real advice. "We would talk and he would tell me things just in conversation or as we were doing different things. But I don't know that I remember or can recall him ever sitting me down and saying like, 'Son, always blah, blah, blah,' or something like that. Certainly he said things like, 'Always respect your mother,' or, 'Always stick up for your brother—you're brothers, you have to love each other.'

"The best advice he may have given us is to stay as a family. My father's very family oriented. He taught me the importance of family and how the family is the most important thing in the world, after God. Your family sticks together. My grandparents were each married over fifty years, until their deaths. "My parents have now been married for fifty years. I've been married for twenty years, and divorce doesn't even creep into my mind. That's just not really part of my thought process, and my parents exemplified that. My father emphasized love, dedication, and commitment to family, to provide for your family and create the best opportunity possible for your children. That's the best advice he gave me through many different ways, through both his words and actions."

As Chris reflects on what his father's legacy will be, he's quick to identify it as productive offspring. "As I mentioned, I've been married twenty years," Chris stated, "and my children are in high school right now and they're doing great academically. They're going to college and they'll go to good colleges. They are productive in every way: they don't have any vices or major flaws. They're not perfect, but they're doing great. My brother has two girls in college and he's successful in his job. My father is the cornerstone of the family, and the architect of all that. I would say family will be his legacy."

THE STORY: UNDERSTANDING WHO IS REALLY IN CHARGE (BY JOE PELLEGRINO)

Debating is great, especially when the debates are passionate and controlled. I once had a man who worked for me, whom we will call Arthur. Arthur was a professed atheist. We would often engage in "spirited" discussions on the topic of faith, him arguing that there was no god and me that there not only is a God but a God who loves each and every one of us. This went on for a few years when something interesting happened to turn the tide.

It happened one morning when all was going smoothly at the weekly newspaper that I co-owned, when suddenly Arthur walked in the front door as white as a ghost. I asked him if he was okay, and he said he needed to speak with me as soon as possible. I invited him into my office and asked him what was wrong. He proceeded to tell me that he had just learned that his mother, whom he loved very much, needed to have, as I remember it, an emergency surgery on her neck that was extremely delicate. I don't remember why, but it was taking its toll on Arthur.

Once he told me this, I asked him if there was anything I could do for him. His response? He asked me to pray for her. As I stated previously, Arthur was a committed atheist, so as I pondered my response the first thing that popped into my mind was to ask him, *Whom would you like me to pray to?* Thankfully I resisted the temptation and simply said I would be happy to pray for her, and that's what we did.

You see, Arthur wasn't an atheist after all, he was just a confused man. It's amazing when confronted with some of the great challenges life offers us, he understood that there needs to be a go-to person to help us through the challenge. Arthur knew I was a man of faith and someone he could trust to help him. Yes, I was his boss, but more importantly I was his friend.

What attracted Arthur to me in that situation had nothing really to do with me, but rather the authority that flowed through me. That is the presence of the Holy Spirit in my life. All too often we complain that there are others in authority over us, but the fact is that it is exactly that structure that helps us to thrive. The key is that the one in authority must be someone we can trust.

THINK ABOUT THIS

Authority is one of those words that we often toss around, but truly see little of it. In Matthew 28:18, Jesus said that all authority in heaven and on earth had been given to Him, and that He would confer that very same authority to others who believed in Him. The first step to receiving authority then is actually acknowledging that Jesus has all authority.

Matthew 7:28–29 is also telling about authority. Jesus had just finished teaching the crowds, and they were amazed at His insights. But here's what I (Joe Pellegrino) find interesting: that passage says that "the crowds were amazed at his teaching, because he taught as one who had authority, and not as their teachers of the law." Scripture makes a distinction between someone who just teaches and Jesus as someone who had authority to say what He did. It appears that the crowd sensed that Jesus had the *right* to say what He did, and not merely the title to say things like the teachers of the law.

The Roman centurion in Matthew 8 understood that fact, which is why he could come to Jesus to ask for healing for his servant. He was a man used to sensing who had authority; he could spot the phonies, or the posers. It is interesting that he came to Jesus and understood immediately how authority works. You merely have to say something and the one under authority knows to believe it or do it—without hesitation. That's why Jesus commended him for his faith *and*, I think, for recognizing that when someone who has authority says something, you should simply believe what they say. He affirmed who Jesus was and His authority to do and speak as He did, even better than His own disciples. And certainly better than the Pharisees.

Chris Broussard saw authority in his father. There was not much of a debate. He knew his father had authority, and he respected it and acted on it. My friend saw something in me as well that shouted, *Authority.* That was Jesus in me, speaking through me to Arthur. As disciples of Jesus, fathers have the right to assume authority because Jesus said He has given it to us. May our children not just hear our words, fathers, but understand that our authority to say these things comes from Christ Himself.

THE QUESTION

What person in your life commands authority so that you will heed and respect his or her counsel? What authority does the Bible have in the way you live your day-to-day life?

Jesus Christ

THAT'S MY DAD!

THATISMYDADMOVEMENT.COM

13

KELLY WRIGHT

THE NONEXISTENT FATHER

BACK STORY

Kelly Wright is a general assignment reporter for the Fox News Channel's Washington, D.C., bureau. He is also a cohost on *America's News Headquarters*, which airs on Saturdays, having previously served as a cohost on *Fox & Friends Weekend*. Most recently, however, Wright was inducted into the Martin Luther King Jr. Board of Sponsors at Morehouse College for his "Beyond the Dream" series.

In 2004, Kelly Wright spent nearly three months reporting on the developments in Iraq. He was among the first reporters to cover the Abu Ghraib Prison scandal and the subsequent court martial cases held in Baghdad. And in April 2007, Wright secured an exclusive sit-down with first lady Laura Bush, where she responded to the Virginia Tech massacres, Katrina recovery, and the president's final term.

He began his journalism career in 1977 while serving in the United States Army, and has received numerous awards for his reporting, including two local Emmy Awards for his developing, reporting, and coproducing a documentary and news series on the transatlantic slave trade. Kelly Wright is a graduate of Oral Roberts University in Tulsa, Oklahoma.

THE INTERVIEW

Kelly Wright is an award-winning journalist with Fox News, knowing how to ask all the right questions in uncovering the truth behind the story. His own life has its own unique story of redemption and God's grace. When you ask him about the story of his father, it's nonexistent. He can only define his relationship with his father as "lost."

"I never knew my real father who was a pastor," Kelly stated. "He was never in my life. He died shortly after I turned two years of age, but he was never in my life or my mother's life. Subsequent to that, I grew up pretty much fatherless, except for my stepfather who had been in my life for about three and a half to four years. My mother was pretty much all of what a father should be, and more."

Kelly was the only child in the single parent household until he was thirteen years old, when his mother adopted his sister. Fortunately, his mother was loving, encouraging, nurturing, and a dream caster. Kelly explains: "My mother always cast a vision to make it plain, and as a result of that I grew up as a dreamer and pretty much it came to pass when I went to Oral Roberts

University. Oral Roberts had a message on his desk that said, 'Make no small plans here.' Well, that was my mother, and she basically infused into me that same kind of thinking—to make no small plans with my life, but to try to do bigger and better things, understanding that I was flawed but loved by a perfect God. That's the kind of home I grew up in."

Fathers are absent for many reasons in their child's life. For some it's financial, while for others the reasons are more painful. According to Kelly, "He wasn't there because he raped my mother when she was sixteen. She was a friend of the pastor's wife. My mother really didn't know what brought that on, for this pastor to rape her. She initially thought she may have been the cause of this, and asked herself, 'What did I do?' She was doing what any rational thinking, self-respecting person would have done, and questioned herself. Then she wondered whom she should tell, knowing that if she went to the police, it would be her word against the pillar of the community because he was a member of the clergy and the pastor of a leading church in that particular community."

Kelly believes that his mother did not want to tell her mother what happened because she felt that her mother would have totally overreacted to the situation. "Being pregnant really compounded things for a sixteen-year-old girl who dreamed of becoming a psychiatrist. That dream fizzled days after her seventeenth birthday when she gave birth to me," Kelly said.

He recounted the backstory to all the drama surrounding this event when his mom had a confrontation with his grandmother before he was born. "Mom had returned home one day and saw that her suitcase was in the living room, and she initially thought, 'I guess I'm getting kicked out of the house.' So she asked, 'What's the suitcase for?' My grandmother responded, 'We're going to fly you to Nebraska so you can have an abortion.' It was at that moment that my mother really seized upon what God was doing in her life and said, 'I'm not going anywhere. I'm not having an abortion. God is telling me this is the only child I'll ever have biologically.'"

Kelly's mom did not go through with the abortion, and five days after her seventeenth birthday Kelly was born. The rest of that story is that his mom indeed became a psychiatrist. "She became a counselor to so many young kids throughout the Hagerstown, Maryland, area, helping many of them complete high school to go on to bigger and better things with their lives," Kelly stated. "What she poured into me she also poured into others. She and my stepdad got married, and at one point they tried to have a child, which never happened. As I said, I have a sister who is thirteen years younger than me and she was adopted because my mom saw that she was in an abusive household and rescued her from that situation. My mom successfully raised two children and has produced what I think are two good citizens."

Kelly acknowledges that his father knew he was born, but decided to move out of the area and not deal with the situation. "I have no ill will toward him," he said. "I know that he is deceased now. I hope he died a forgiven man, because we're forgiven of all of our sins, and I hope he died knowing that he was forgiven too. Again, I've just never really thought about not having a father. I had God as my Father. In Isaiah it says that God would never orphan us, and He has never abandoned me or orphaned me. If I can brag about any father, it would be about my heavenly Father who never abandoned me or orphaned me."

Another interesting aspect of Kelly's early years is his name. "Kids were calling me a bastard because I was born illegitimately," Kelly said. "They knew my mother wasn't married, and my father was not around. So my stepfather, being sensitive to that, said, 'Okay, let me go ahead and do this legally since we're already married. Let's put Wright on his name,' because my original name was Kelvin Andre Overton. That's how I'm Kelly Wright.

"I know a lot of people in this day and age talk about fatherless children who are doomed for failure and destined for bad things. I'm living proof that it ain't necessarily so, as a Broadway musical once put it. It really depends on who your mother is, and I'm not the only person like that. Dr. Ben Carson and his brother were raised by their mom after she went through a divorce. The power of a mother can change your life. In fact, the power of any caring parent can change a life. That's what my mother did and that's what Dr. Ben Carson's mother did for him. Of course, we know his history of becoming a great doctor. He could have joined a gang, but his mother instilled in him a desire to read even though she didn't know how to read.

"I'm just grateful to Christ, who infused in my mother with this tenacity and perseverance and clarity of thought to weather every storm as a single parent, despite the obvious difficulties. Everything that I accomplish, I owe to June Lorraine Overton Wright, my mother. And, as it happens, once I was born I became the apple of my grandmother's eye—the one who wanted to have me aborted. It just shows you the completeness of God. No, I never have second thoughts about my natural father. I always have thoughts about my heavenly Father."

Kelly's teen years were rough, as he has indicated. He was hanging with the wrong crowd, so his mother saw to it that he went to the top school in Washington, DC, at that time, Gonzaga, which cost a pretty penny. "I was just drifting toward mediocrity because I wanted to be cool like the rest of the kids," Kelly said. "What my mother did was show some courage there as well. She stepped in when the school was going to pass me on the D average and said, 'No, he will not be taught how to be mediocre; he will not be taught how to just skate by. I'm going to keep him back. He's going to repeat the ninth grade and we're leaving the school.' Well, that's pretty dramatic, isn't it?

"She moved me back to Hagerstown from Washington, and put me in a school that was not going to settle for mediocre. I remember her driving me out to the school, and on the way saying, 'Now, you're not going to go to any of the public schools here. We're not going to have that. We're going to expose you to this school. You're going to be a dominating black student in this school. You will have no problem accepting your white friends and they will have no problems accepting you because I've taught you how to respect people for the content of their character, not the color of their skin. You're proud of your heritage and you're going to make us look good.' And she was right. I went to the school and flourished.

"I became an honor student throughout high school, and started working in radio. I became the student body president, and then from there went to college at Oral Roberts University. After ORU, I joined the military, where I went through some difficult days that led to me getting an ill-advised marriage. I was married for four years and have a wonderful daughter from that marriage who is a joy in my heart and a delight to my soul. But during that period of going through the divorce and leaving the army, I went through some difficult times and ended up living in my car on the streets of Atlanta, Georgia. I went from being a United States soldier, a college-educated man, a sergeant in the army, working as a news anchor and reporter in Savannah, Georgia, to losing my job and living on the streets.

"Needless to say, I wasn't welcome in Atlanta, Georgia, so we moved down to Montgomery, Alabama, and that's where my prodigal experience comes to a close. I realized in Montgomery that I was at a place where Rosa Parks stood against racial injustice. I was at a place where Martin Luther King Jr. had begun to launch an incredible nonviolent movement that would change the course of history in America. I remember being a child looking up to him and hoping that someday I could live like him or emulate him and speak the way he spoke in terms of building bridges that would bring us close together as a people. I began to think, 'What am I doing on the streets of Montgomery, selling fake leather goods when there's so much more to be done?' That's when I began to hear God's voice clearly and simply saying, 'You can always go home.'

"I was thinking, 'Well, I have to clean up my mess before I go home,' and God was just saying, 'You can always go home.' So I said, 'I'm just not doing all the things that my mother taught me and that You've taught me—I'm struggling.' Then God said again, 'You can always go home, dummy.' And I was like, 'Okay. I get it now. If You're going to talk to me like that, God, I think I need to pay attention and go home.'

"I remember it was getting close to Christmas and I was thinking about my mother and the decorations that were always around our house during Christmastime, the scent of the Christmas tree, the pine, and Johnny Mathis singing Christmas carols on my mother's stereo—the beauty of the Christmas season. So I dropped off all the leather goods in Atlanta, Georgia, and thanked the gentleman who had hired me, and he wished me the best. He actually was happy to see me finally making a decision to go home.

"As soon I got home, it was like the prodigal son, but with my mother standing there with open arms—she welcomed me in and embraced me. Being typical June, her nature, she said, 'Welcome home. I love you. I'm so glad you're back. I'm so excited that you're here. I'm happy for you. By the way, I got a job interview for you at the local TV station next week.' With that look of assurance, casting that vision, she looked at me and said, 'And you will get that job.' And that is exactly what I did, and I've never looked back."

THE STORY: TIM TEBOW (BY JOE PELLEGRINO)

In a recent e-mail, I read about a woman named Pam, who knows the pain of considering abortion. More than twenty-four years ago, she and her husband, Bob, were serving as missionaries to the Philippines and praying for a fifth child. Pam contracted amoebic dysentery, an infection of the intestine caused by a parasite found in contaminated food or drink. She went into a coma and was treated with strong antibiotics before they discovered that she was pregnant.

The doctors urged her to abort the baby for her own safety, and told her that the medicines had caused irreversible damage to her baby. She refused the abortion and cited her Christian faith as the reason for her hope that her son would be born without the devastating disabilities the physicians predicted. Pam said the doctors didn't think of him as a life; rather, they thought of him as a mass of fetal tissue.

While pregnant, Pam nearly lost their baby four times but still refused to consider abortion. She recalled making a pledge to God with her husband: "If You will give us a son, we'll name him Timothy and we'll make him a preacher."

Pam spent the last two months of her pregnancy in bed and eventually gave birth to a healthy baby boy on August 14, 1987. Pam's youngest son is indeed a preacher. He preaches in prisons, makes hospital visits, and serves with his father's ministry in the Philippines. He also plays professional football. Pam's son is Tim Tebow.

The University of Florida's star quarterback became the first sophomore in history to win college football's highest award, the Heisman Trophy. Though his NFL career has been off and on, it has provided an incredible platform for his Christian witness. Tim's notoriety and the family's inspiring story have given Pam numerous opportunities to speak on behalf of women's centers across the country. Pam Tebow believes that every little baby saved matters.

THINK ABOUT THIS

Like many missionaries, Pam and Bob were excited to follow their calling in their mission field, which was in the Philippines. During their tenure there, Pam contracted an infection called amoebic dysentery, which is caused by a parasite found in contaminated food or drink. Bob, Pam's husband, who had often prayed with Pam for a fifth child, found himself praying for something else altogether: his wife's life. The infection put Pam into a coma for which she was treated with strong antibiotics. As doctors worked to treat the infection, a new discovery was made: Pam was pregnant. And we know that baby has grown up into a man who is a faithful witness for Jesus Christ.

God's promises are always backed up with a plan. Pam and Bob decided to trust in God's promise, as did Kelly's mom. They allowed God's plan for both Tim and Kelly to unfold as God saw fit, not as the world would decide for them. And because of Tim's parents and Kelly's mom, who chose life instead of abortion, many people have now been blessed because of their boys' presence in the world.

THE QUESTION

Without God, many people wind up completely and utterly lost. What decision can you make today that will lead you out of the wilderness of relationships?

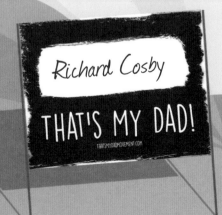

Richard Cosby

THAT'S MY DAD!

THATSMYDADMOVEMENT.COM

14

RITA COSBY

THE COURAGEOUS FATHER

BACK STORY

Rita Cosby is one of the most recognized and respected broadcasters in America. Born in Brooklyn, she is a renowned Emmy-winning television host, veteran correspondent, and multiple best-selling author, who has anchored highly rated primetime shows on Fox News Channel and MSNBC. She is currently a special correspondent for the top-rated CBS syndicated newsmagazine, *Inside Edition*, and does frequent hosting and reporting for CNN/HLN, and hosts *The Rita Cosby Show* on the legendary WABC Radio, the most listened to talk station in America.

Named as one of the Most Influential Women in Radio

in both 2014 and 2015 by *Radio Ink Magazine*, she was also honored in 2015 with two prestigious Gracie Awards for Outstanding Host and Outstanding Talk Show. Honors for the three-time Emmy winner include the Matrix Award, Headliner Award, and Jack Anderson Award for journalism excellence. A recipient of the Ellis Island Medal of Honor and the Lech Walesa Freedom Award, she hosts the National Memorial Day Parade broadcast to all US military installations around the world.

Rita Cosby has written back-to-back *New York Times* bestsellers. Her most recent one, *Quiet Hero: Secrets from My Father's Past,* details her fascinating discovery about her own father, a Nazi prisoner of war, who was saved by American troops during World Word II.

THE INTERVIEW

Rita Cosby is an Emmy Award-winning television host, veteran correspondent, and journalist, having covered many major events during her illustrious career with Fox News Channel, MSNBC, and CNN. Among them is that she was the first American journalist to interview Pope Francis. But her greatest revelation as a journalist was learning of her father's remarkable story as a Polish resistance fighter during World War II. It was later on in her life when he informed her that, as a teenager in Warsaw, Poland, he was thrust into World War II when the Nazis invaded his homeland.

"My father was a humble man, as he never spoke a word about his own heroism when I was growing up," Rita recalled. "But the visible scars etched all over his body spoke volumes. He survived the unimaginable and never spoke about what he'd seen or experienced until his final years."

She went on to say, "Now I know why my father taught me at an early age to be fearless, not be afraid to take chances, and to stand up for what you believe in. He would tell me he could always live with himself by trying and possibly failing, but he could never live with himself for never trying something important. His life exemplified sheer courage and unwavering determination. That was the best advice he ever gave me.

"At the age of fifteen, as his family was Polish Catholic, they could've covertly snuck my dad out of the country to a relative in Switzerland. Instead, my dad willingly decided to stay and fight for his country in the Polish resistance. He told his mother, 'I would rather die with friends than live with strangers. Poland and freedom are worth fighting for.' To have that kind of moral compass and love of country, especially at that young age, is most extraordinary to me, especially given the fact that his country was being obliterated at the hands of the Nazis and the odds of surviving the onslaught of Hitler's madness was extremely low.

"Today's millennial generation of fifteen-year-olds are armed with iPads and cell phones. My dad saw the death of his friends who, like him, were making Molotov cocktails, firing stolen guns with few bullets, and stood ready to take on one of the most brutal war machines in world history."

Rita realizes that it was that steely determination of fighting against all odds that made her dad never afraid to speak up for what he believed in. "If he saw a neighbor being mistreated, he spoke out," she said. "If he saw someone maligning America or not appreciating the small things in life, he stood strong and let his voice be heard. He knew what it was like to lose everything, including his freedom. He knew firsthand the contempt Nazi soldiers had for their prisoners as he was but ninety pounds and six feet tall when he escaped from Stalag IV-B and was rescued by American troops."

That DNA has served Rita well over the many years in her work as a journalist. "All my life, I have always relished new opportunities and, like my father, I've never been afraid to try and go beyond even my own expectations," she stated. "Whether it's reaching out to a rogue world leader for an interview, a key newsmaker who lives thousands of miles away, or accepting a position at a start-up network called Fox News."

Rita was one of the first wave of journalists who launched with Fox News in 1995, taking a chance with an upstart company, eschewing other offers at more established networks, which would have been more practical. "I took Fox because it sounded new and bold," she said, "and it ended up being one of the greatest decisions of my life as I became a host and senior correspondent. I traveled the world with some of the finest news crews I've ever known, meeting world leaders and many others in far corners of the globe. I often left with the clothes on my back covering a breaking news story, and ended up covering a dozen or more other stories by the time I came home weeks or months later. I learned to enjoy every moment and truly got my sense of adventure from my father. I also learned persistence, to not accept no for an answer if it is truly something I want to do."

Rita's father and mother came to America in 1956 with a hundred dollars between them, like many immigrants ready to start a brand-new life together, learn a new language, and explore a new land. "He said taking the *Queen Mary* over to America was one of the most exciting times in his life. He was not afraid, but full of optimism and hope as they arrived in New York Harbor."

Rita was born in Brooklyn, New York, and raised in Greenwich, Connecticut, with her older brother, Alan. She remembers pleasant childhood memories that involve camping trips with her family in their beat-up white Chrysler station wagon to picturesque Somes Sound View Campground on Mount Desert Island in Maine. "My parents loved the outdoors, where birds soared high above us," Rita recalled, "and we'd go on long hikes picking wild blueberries, go on canoe rides, or roast marshmallows by a campfire. My parents always enjoyed the family being together and the simple things of life; never any fancy dinners or fancy shopping trips, just spending time, exploring the surrounding wilderness with one another in simple surroundings. My dad was a true survivalist, and my brother and I had to learn how to survive. We had to keep up with him, or at least try our hardest to do so."

Those family trips and their father's adventurous spirit made her and her brother rather equal in what they had to do to survive those wilderness outings. "I think my father forgot I was a young girl, so he cut my hair one time shorter than my brother's and often had us both load the canoe or have us paddle along the waterway for miles on end," she said. "We often had blisters from all the paddling, and even if they drew blood, that wouldn't halt the journey. There was no quitting in my family, even if it came to an afternoon canoe ride down large rapids at a pretty good clip and no food or water on board. It was boot camp at an early age, mentally and physically, which certainly left no time for complaining."

Her father's heroism during the war was greatly inspired by his mother, Rita's grandmother, whom she never met because she passed away soon after the war, well before Rita was born.

"My dad always had great respect for women, especially his own mother," Rita said. "In his final years, while he shared with me his grueling life during the war, he became very emotional when we discussed his mother, whom he thought was truly heroic. He said she really kept the family together and calm in the most difficult of circumstances, as Nazi bombs bombarded their city. She also was a stalwart woman of faith. A devout Catholic, she kept a hidden altar in the basement of their apartment, which was strictly forbidden under Nazi rule.

"Every time their apartment was destroyed by bombs, she'd create a new altar in the next temporary home. She frequently told my father that nothing would destroy her faith, not even the brutal Nazi regime. Rather than turning over her radio at one point, as getting news from the outside world was also forbidden, she instead threw it out of the window and smashed it. She was unwavering in her love of her country, her family, and her faith. I never met her, but I feel I know her well through my father's tears as we visited his homeland and her gravesite in 2009. It was his first visit back home since the war, and I could see he was heartbroken to have never seen her again after the Warsaw uprising began in late 1944. He loved and truly admired his mother and her courage."

It's no surprise that one of Rita's favorite memories of being with her father had to do with endurance and commitment—when he ran marathons. "Meeting him at the ten- and twenty-mile mark of many marathons, I would always meet him there at both key points and hand him his Gatorade and a towel. He always looked so strong, incredibly determined, and even at the twenty-mile mark, he was always ready to finish the final six miles, even if it was partly uphill and a sweltering hot day. He was a true champion in every sense of the word, completing a remarkable thirty-three marathons in his lifetime, and even winning the Marine Corps Marathon in Washington, DC, in the seventy-and-older age group one year.

"I was always so proud of him when I'd see him charging at the twenty-mile mark. Even if he was exhausted, he never showed it or said it. All he kept saying was, 'I must keep going; I cannot stop. I am finishing this race no matter what. Can't take breaks.' Then he would huff on. That epitomized who he was, no matter what hurdle was thrown at him. He was focused on the goal and finished his task.

"One time after he had passed out right after finishing the Boston Marathon, he recovered quickly and his first comments focused on how this hardship would only make him a better runner, and more prepared the next time. He took setbacks as life's lessons to make one better.

"Between all the marathons and many decades of intense training, my father took great pride in telling me that distance-wise, he'd remarkably 'run around the equator two and a half times.' In thinking about this, he was remarkably strong, both mentally and physically, maintained a healthy regimen, and was a fighter to the end. He was always in pursuit of the 'run' and always ready to take up a challenge to lead. It was not surprising to me that at the end of my dad's life, despite many of his organs failing, his heart was strong and powerful."

Learning life's lessons were certainly part of the Cosby household, which inspired Rita to always treat others with respect and not complain about hard work. Her father relished challenges, and this mind-set found fertile soil in young Rita's life that would serve her well later on as she embarked on her career as a journalist. Most importantly, her father taught her to "spend time focused on the mission, what matters, and not sweat the small stuff. He also taught her that you must work as a team, as he did in battle, and respect people of all levels."

Her work as a journalist would require these interpersonal traits. "I know a good broadcast involves many people far beyond me, as the on-air person," she said. "There are so many talented people whose faces you don't see and who absolutely play a key role in making a great story or show on television or radio. Broadcasting and life are team sports. I also know any bad day I might have will never be as difficult as what my father endured. Any hurdles I encounter seem small compared to my father's life, and I am grateful for great friends and colleagues and work I love to do. I am deeply passionate and loyal to friends and colleagues, and I get that determination and bond of friendship from my father. My father had to trust his young friends with his life in battle. When he was severely injured by a mortar shell, his comrades dragged his body onto a makeshift stretcher and carried him through heavy German sniper fire, which is truly a sign of unwavering loyalty to your comrade whom they refused to leave behind."

Rita's "quiet hero" left a great legacy, not just for Rita and her family, but also for the many others who came after him in a liberated Poland. Rita memorialized her dad's story in her *New York Times* best-selling book *Quiet Hero*, which they were able to write together soon before he passed away in 2012. "I remember the greatest call in my life was telling my dad that the book about his life made the *New York Times* best-seller list. I said, 'Congrats, Dad!' But he got it right away that the book's success had meaning far beyond his own life. He immediately replied, 'Congrats to Poland and to my colleagues who never lived to tell their stories, and congrats to the American troops who saved me and are being recognized for their heroism. I am so glad the world is learning about them now.'

"He was humble yet passionate to the end. One of the last things my dad did was sign an autograph in the hospital as he was on his deathbed with cancer, as many people had seen him in TV interviews with me or read our book. My father always felt awkward when he was asked to sign something or take a photo, but he came to understand that it meant they appreciated those who fought for freedom, that it represented something greater than any one person.

"In retrospect, it was also courageous of my father to ultimately share his painful war years with me to do the book, thereby having to relive some painful moments he had hoped to never recount again. It was truly a redemptive experience, where he faced his fears and returned with me to his homeland of Poland, back to the very streets where many of his comrades were killed. At one point, my father fell to his knees, overcome with emotion, at the very scene where a devastating explosion killed virtually his entire unit in a single instant.

"To this day, I often think that his return to Warsaw to relive those painful and deeply traumatic experiences was one of the most courageous things he ever did. He did it because he wanted people, especially young people, to understand that freedom is not free and is always worth fighting for. I think of my father every time I see a young GI in uniform, or when I see a warrior back from multiple deployments. I can better understand their physical and emotional struggles after dealing with it so intimately with my own father who was physically and emotionally scarred."

Rita's dad lived the American dream, becoming a successful and well-respected civil engineer in America, building highways and bridges, additions to the Library of Congress, the Dirksen Senate Office Building, the National Gallery of Art in DC, and more. His ultimate legacy will undoubtedly be tied to the journey of a father and daughter who was to become one of America's top broadcast journalists, and the rediscovery of family and everything meaningful during the last years of his life.

"My father truly had an extraordinary life from ultimate survival as a teenager until about sixty-five years later. Many in Poland thought he died during the war. But after the Polish leaders discovered he was still alive, he received one of the highest honors from the president of Poland for his bravery in the Warsaw uprising. My father, who never sought attention or fame, was treated like a rock star by the people of Poland, and that meant so much to both of us, as it meant his sacrifice and that of his comrades was not forgotten.

"He also addressed the Daughters of the American Revolution in Constitution Hall in Washington, DC, and got a standing ovation after talking about the heroic women who fought alongside him in battle. One of those fighters was his cousin, Rita, who was a sharpshooter during the war, whom I was named after.

"My father died knowing he made a difference, and had no regrets, and that was a tremendous gift and model for how I believe we should all live our lives. When I addressed the American Legion national convention soon after his death, I said that I hoped that all veterans are treated like rock stars and signing autographs at the end of their lives. If my father's story has encouraged others to appreciate our military and their families' sacrifice, then my father would say all the heartache he endured was worth it. I may not pick up guns or Molotov cocktails like my father, but I am armed with a loud microphone and pen, and vow for the rest of my life to fight for people and stories I believe need to be told."

THE STORY: THE PORTRAIT OF A MAN
(BY JOE PELLEGRINO, JR)

For as long as I can remember, my grandfather, John Pellegrino, was the picture of the postmodern classification of an old man. John was a gentleman of sorts, but perhaps a bit rougher than that. Old-fashioned and giving off a strong vibe of 1940s nostalgia, he clearly felt lost in the current decade. He exhibited a boring, sedated attitude toward those whom he was uncomfortable with and toward those he knew he showed just as little emotion. He was a man whose heart loved but whose actions did not show it. John was a man of few words and, as it seemed, a few feelings.

I came up with this view of John Pellegrino about the moment I was first reprimanded by him for sitting on the "good couches" in his Jersey Shore home. I was upset, annoyed, and terrified of this old man. In visits after that, I tiptoed tentatively around him and only spoke to him when it was necessary. But about the time I entered into junior high school, I began to come to the understanding that this John Pellegrino, whom I called Poppy, was a man whose life stretched way beyond the short period of time that I had known him. As I explored the idea that perhaps there was more to Poppy than met the eye, I began to find out the full story of this man as pages were studied and walls were broken down. The more I learned, the more I loved. In the final several years of his life, I met the real John Pellegrino. For the first time ever, I realized that my grandfather had once been the portrait of a man.

I stumbled across an old photo album, not long ago, filled with old pictures from a much simpler time. As I thumbed through the grainy images that were clearly processed no less than fifty years before, I noticed that several of them featured the beaming face of Poppy. He was quite a bit younger looking with rosy cheeks and dark curly hair. I continued to look through the pictures until I found one that changed my relationship with Poppy forever. He was walking out of a New Jersey train station carrying a bag, wearing a World War II uniform. On his face was a smile that indicated this was his homecoming. As I studied the photograph, my heart began to swell with emotion as I realized who my grandfather was. I had known that he had served in the war, but, as it seemed, so had every grandfather. But there was something in this picture that brought on a new perspective. Not long after that, I found myself in the previously awkward situation of sitting alone with Poppy. As he stared into space, I sat up and asked plainly, "What was it like when you were young?" He looked at me, and then, as if someone had turned a switch on in the man's head, he began to rattle off to me excitedly about his life.

For a moment I had lost track of the man I was speaking with. Was this the same John Pellegrino I had known? He explained to me everything from the early 1930s where he and his family suffered through the Great Depression. He told me a story about his father cooking his pet rabbit out of desperation for food. But even as hard as the times he experienced were, he lit up as he spoke of his past.

Finally coming to the war, he spoke of his friends and the places he had been. He was an army sergeant, proud to be serving his country. For several years he fought, leaving his fiancée, Gloria, back home to await their marriage. Just before the war's completion, my grandfather was shot in the leg in France and sent home with an honorable discharge. He came home bearing a Purple Heart, and that brought us to the day of the homecoming photograph, which my father calls sentimentally "When Johnny Comes Marching Home."

After the war, Poppy raised up a family with my Nanny. They lived the common American life, struggling at times but altogether providing necessities for their family. He told me of the job he had for many years at Lever Brothers, and that the only vacation he had taken was to Scottsdale, Arizona. His eyes twinkled as he recalled his clearly full and well-lived life. I had never seen my Poppy talk in such a way before. For that matter, I had never really seen him talk very much at all. The way he came alive that day stayed with me, even though he would rarely come alive like that after that time. Perhaps the final appearance of the real John Pellegrino was at the wedding of his granddaughter, Alexis, in November of 2005. Following that, it was a steep decline.

The feelings for my grandfather lay dormant in my heart during that time of decline. I loved him as always, yes, but I had forgotten what I knew of him. I watched him suffer through the final years of his life, weakened by age and crippled by poor health. It was a sad sight to see, a man knowing he is at the end of his life. He looked nothing like the man in the pictures. Poppy died less than three years after the wedding in May of 2008. It was not until his funeral late that month that I found myself remembering again the real John Pellegrino. As I stood at his wake and watched a slideshow of photographs from his life, I was suddenly moved to tears. The final picture that flashed on the screen was the famous "When Johnny Comes Marching Home" picture. In the background played the song for which it was named.

Just then, I was overcome with a feeling of pride and respect for my grandfather, John Pellegrino, the picture of a patriot and the portrait of a man. I was nearly ready to salute the screen. I glanced from the casket where he lay lifeless and back to the screen where he was projected in his prime, slowly shaking my head at the concept of aging. How could they be the same? How could a man who lived such a noble life be reduced to this? Where did Johnny go? My father, John's son, came up behind me and put his hand on my shoulder. I looked up at him and begged of him just that question. As I welled up, the slideshow concluded with a short clip of Nanny and Poppy dancing at Alexis' wedding just three years prior. *There you are, Johnny,* I thought.

It has been nearly a year since Poppy died. Every time I see a soldier on the news, every time I watch the Military Channel, every time I pass by a military base, I think of my grandfather. Whenever I hear of the Purple Heart, whether in conversation or in a movie, I think of Poppy. And whenever I see a man living for the sake of his family, I think of John Pellegrino.

THINK ABOUT THIS

Courage is in short supply in our day and age, when people would rather conform to politically correct agendas and not stand up for what they truly believe. As my (Joe Battaglia) friend Pastor Rick Warren recently said in one of his sermons: "It's the veterans, not the reporters, who give us freedom of the press. It's the veterans, not the poets, who give us freedom of speech. It's veterans, not political organizers, who give us the freedom to assemble. It's veterans, not lawyers, who give us the freedom to a fair trial. It's veterans, not politicians, who give us the freedom to vote. And it is veterans, not preachers, who give us the freedom to worship publicly. So on behalf of a grateful nation, thank you."

Maybe the reason honesty and courage are rare commodities today is that so few of those in charge of anything in this country had to fight for their freedom. Things have more worth when there's more risk in achieving them.

I remember a line in a recent western called *Range War*, starring two of my favorite actors, Robert Duvall and Kevin Costner. In short, the two of them, crusty old cowboys with honor, decided to stand up to the typical gang of bad guys who thought nothing of stealing and killing the weak and innocent to get what they wanted. In one scene, in the local saloon, one scared citizen cautioned the Costner character that doing what he was doing could cost him his life. Costner replied with this line: "There are things that gnaw at a man's soul worse than dying."

I don't know who wrote that script, but kudos to him or her for coming up with that line. Rita Cosby's father and my grandfather understood that courage often comes with a price. That's why it's worth so much today—because it's so rare.

THE QUESTION

What's gnawing at your soul today? What do you need to stand up for despite the risks or the dangers that may follow? Remember, your children are watching you. They want to know that you'd be willing to pay any price for standing up for them.

15

RESOURCE

THE POWER OF FATHERS SAY

Men are being pulled in so many ways today that distract them from their primary roles as husbands and fathers. As a result, all too often our children suffer. Now more than ever before, we need to understand the true role dads play in their children's lives as our kids face a world we could have never imagined. This is where Fathers Say comes in. Fathers Say is a powerful resource to teach men the power of their words, the impact of offering their blessing to a child, and the difference mentoring can make in that child's life. What fathers say can determine their child's way.

Let's turn every day into fathers say by continually blessing and mentoring our children, grandchildren, or a child in need. Fathers Say is a program *anyone* can do, whether individually or in a group setting. The difference it can make in your life, family, and the community you live in is incredible. All you have to do is use it. Change will come, guaranteed!

Are you ready? There are three steps to meaningful change in your fathering: engage, encourage, and equip. Let's quickly look at each.

ENGAGE

The Power of the Blessing

What is this thing called a "blessing"? It's not complex. In fact, it's pretty straightforward. It's a word of approval or a word of support. It's a word that bestows confidence, hope, and a sense of well-being. And it brings affirmation. It's a word that allows a young child or adult to move forward boldly, humbly, with courage and confidence, into the future. It's a word that says, *You are a masterpiece that has been created for a unique purpose in this life.* It's a word that helps our children, our family, our friends, and those we work with know they are valuable and fashioned for something special in this life.

Some of us have received a blessing, but many of us have not. Several years ago at one of our men's conferences, we gave a call for men who felt they had never experienced a blessing from their parents, family, or anyone, particularly from their dads, to come forward. To our amazement, the majority of those present came forward—men from their teens well into their seventies.

When we see people who are excelling in life, regardless of their family's financial or economic status, we often will find folks who come from a loving, supportive, encouraging family background who continually imparted words of blessing into their lives. They were told they could do anything they set their heart and mind to. Studies have shown that many super successful people who came from difficult and distressed families and backgrounds made it in life because of the words of blessing spoken to them.

You may be saying, *I never had such affirming words spoken to me.* In fact, you may have heard nothing but discouraging, demeaning, angry, and abusive words directed to you. Whatever the case may be, you can still learn how to be a person who blesses everyone in your life. Many of us didn't learn about the power of blessing until late in life—which means it is not too late. This is what Fathers Say is all about.

ENCOURAGE

Now that you understand the power of the blessing and the importance of being a dad, how do you begin to implement what you have learned in this book? The ideal situation is an actively engaged dad. The other end of the spectrum, however, is a father who has been alienated from his children. Some kids have no father figure at all, or someone else stands in the father role for that child. Providing a blessing works in all of these cases, regardless of the situation they are in. It all starts with understanding the importance of your words.

Four Ways to Memorialize the Blessing

There are four ways to memorialize the blessing you give to your child. You can create a professional video, shoot a homemade video using a webcam or video camera, make an audio recording, or simply write a letter by hand. If you choose to make a video, an audio recording, or a handwritten letter, remember that none of these have to be extremely polished. They only need to be sincere.

What should you say in your blessing? Well, we are glad you asked. Your blessing should include a greeting, where you open up on a positive note and are sure to personalize it with their name. You'll want to make sure to talk about the relationship you have with the child. If the relationship has been less than ideal, then simply ask for forgiveness and promise to do better. But remember that if you promise, then you need to keep your word. Then spend some time affirming the child. This can be through talking about what makes the child unique, how much they have value, and speak specifically to his or her purpose and their ability to achieve it. Then simply end by telling then that you love them and you will be there for them. If you are recording this for a child you don't know that well or at all, then use the time to introduce yourself and speak encouragement into their lives.

The truth is that you don't have to be the child's father to bless a child. In many situations, the child's natural father is unwilling or unable to perform this blessing, which is why you are needed. What is important is that the child hears words of wisdom, encouragement, and affirmation from a father figure in his or her life. If at all possible, the ideal way to do this is face-to-face. We understand, however, that this may not always be possible.

EQUIP

Now that you've spoken the blessing, what's next? What comes after that? It is time to effectively mentor them.

If you have children, mentoring is taking place daily. How? By them watching your every move! Effective mentoring is designed to understand this truth and making the adjustments necessary to truly bless your kids through an intentional mentoring process.

If you do not have your own children, or are just thinking about mentoring a boy who is in need, then the term *mentoring* can be intimidating. Some men think they are not equipped to mentor another man or boy. But when you truly boil down mentoring, it's all about being there for another guy, listening to his challenges, asking him questions, and doing your best to point him in the right direction. The following components are key to successful mentoring and the building of long-lasting relationships.

Who should you mentor?

As a rule of thumb you should only mentor those who are the same gender as yourself. Of course, there are exceptions to this rule, such as if you are the child's mom or dad.

The First Meeting or Phone Call

As you begin the relationship, it's always best to let the person you are mentoring talk about themselves. Get to know each other and then set a consistent meeting schedule. For example, every Thursday at 7:00 a.m., or the first Monday of each month. The important thing is to block out a specific day and time that both of you agree on, trying to keep it as consistent as possible.

Open with Accountability Questions

Establish a routine for the meetings. We suggest that you begin by asking a set of accountability questions each time you meet. These questions should be direct and to the point. Your child or the one you are mentoring will come to the meeting expecting you to ask them these questions. Stress to them the importance of answering honestly each and every time. If you need to dig deeper on any one question, make a note of it, but continue to have the one being mentored answer all of the questions before digging deeper on any one question. Once all of the questions are answered, then you can go back to any of his answers and explore them further.

Listen Intently to Their Answers

As you listen to their answers, do not judge or show shock at what they are saying to you. In all situations, extend and reflect grace, which is very important if you are to gain his trust. You may also find yourself wanting to interrupt them while they are speaking, but I caution you to resist this urge. Instead, let them get everything out and then ask questions when they are done.

Ask Questions, Questions, and More Questions

The art of asking good questions is a powerful tool indeed. On our website there is a tool called The Value of Questions, which was offered by John Maxwell's Maximum Impact Club (mileaderonline.com). If you can master this art, you won't have to come up with very many solutions for them. Instead, the questions you ask them should make them realize what they should do. Again, this art takes time to refine, but this is the end goal.

Provide Positive and Negative Motivations

As you are listening to your mentee answer the questions, start thinking about some positive or negative motivations you can provide for them. These are dependent on their answers and are framed as a question. For example, a positive motivation would be to ask them, "What do you have to gain in life by avoiding these temptations? Instead of giving into this temptation, what kind of person do you want to become?" An example of negative motivation would be to ask them, "If you continue doing this over and over again, what do you stand to lose in your life?"

Recognize When Someone Is in Need of Additional Help

Remember you are not a counselor; you are a dad or a friend. I repeat this again: you are not a counselor. That means if someone is talking of suicide or harming themselves, talking about harming someone else, or is becoming visibly aggressive or agitated, then you should arrange for them to speak with a professional counselor.

Be Patient

Patience is truly a virtue, so make sure you extend it to others. Remember some of the young people you will be mentoring might be coming from a bad place and will try to test you to see why you are doing this. Or it could be that they just have a bad attitude. Therefore, patience is key. Don't quit. Ultimately, you will become an important person in their lives.

GET STARTED TODAY

Procrastination is a great challenge for many people—we see others who need help but we just fail to act. Think for a moment if you were there for another person, young or old, and your mentoring helped them to overcome a great challenge in their life or put them on the right path—what's that worth? Look for an opportunity to serve another and seize the moment. To see sample Fathers Say videos or to obtain mentoring resources, please visit www.FathersSay.com.

EPILOGUE

AN EXAMPLE FOR THE AGES

In our Introduction, we asserted that the greatest Father-child relationship is between God the Father and His Son Jesus Christ. Jesus sums up this relationship best in John 3:16, which may be the most familiar verse in the Bible: "For God so loved the world that he gave his one and only Son, that whoever believes in him shall not perish but have eternal life." This verse is not just about salvation or the offer of eternal life. If we stop there, then we'll miss the additional significance contained in this verse. A more careful study reveals something deeper about the nature of God's love that as fathers, we would do well to heed .

Simply, fatherly love gives. "For God so loved the world that he *gave*." In order to best express itself, love must give. In fact, it is not love if it's self-contained. Jesus warns us that hoarding things for ourselves is not just selfish, but also so unlike God. If we seek to become more like Him, then we must give, just as He gave. And when we give of ourselves, we parallel the actions of God the Father, who gave of Himself because His nature demanded it. God so loved His creation to such a degree that He was willing to sacrifice His Son in order to reclaim it. What a great lesson to impart to us: sacrifice is part of being a good father.

As fathers, our love for our children will always be there to remind them that someone really knows them, someone cares for them, and someone loves them unconditionally. The Father's love gives, and does so sacrificially.

Today, if you haven't told your children that you love them, why not plan to do that before the day is over? It may be the one thing your children needed to hear today that may change their lives!

JOIN THE MOVEMENT!

ThatsMyDadMovement.com

AND BE PART OF THE SOLUTION!